D1669062

Resurrection Of The Dead

by Derek Prince

"If by any means I might attain unto the resurrection of the dead."

Philippians 3:11

ISBN 0-934920-05-2

TABLE OF CONTENTS

DEREK PRINCE

King's Scholar, Eton College
B.A., M.A. Cambridge
Formerly
Fellow of King's College,
Cambridge

ABOUT THE AUTHOR

Derek Prince was born in India, of British parents. He was educated as a scholar of Greek and Latin at two of Britain's most famous educational institutions - Eton College and Cambridge University. From 1940 to 1949, he held a Fellowship (equivalent to a resident professorship) in Ancient and Modern Philosophy at King's College, Cambridge. He also studied Hebrew and Aramaic, both at Cambridge University and at the Hebrew University in Jerusalem. In addition, he speaks a number of other modern languages.

In the early years of World War II, while serving as a hospital attendant with the British Army, Derek Prince experienced a life-changing encounter with Jesus Christ, concerning which, he writes:

> Out of this encounter, I formed two conclusions which I have never since had reason to change: first, that Jesus Christ is alive; second, that the Bible is a true, relevant, up-to-date book. These two conclusions radically and permanently altered the whole course of my life.

At the end of World War II, he remained where the British Army had placed him - in Jerusalem. Through his marriage to his first wife, Lydia, he became father to the eight adopted girls in Lydia's children's home there. Together, the family saw the rebirth of the State of Israel in 1948.

While serving as educator in Kenya, Derek and Lydia adopted their ninth child, an African baby girl. Lydia died in 1975, and Derek Prince married his present wife, Ruth, in 1978.

In the intervening years, Derek Prince has served as pastor, educator, lecturer, and counselor on several continents, and is internationally recognized as one of the leading Bible expositors of our time. He has authored over 20 books, many of which have been translated into other languages. In great demand as a conference speaker, Derek Prince travels frequently to many other parts of the world, and also maintains a base in Israel.

Non-denominational and non-sectarian in his approach, Derek Prince has prophetic insight into the significance of current events in the light of Bible prophecy.

*   *   *   *   *

With a few changes, these messages are printed here exactly as they were delivered over the air on the Study Hour radio program.

I
At The End Of Time

Eternity: The Realm Of God's Being—God's Two Universal Appointments After Death: Resurrection And Judgment

Welcome to the Study Hour.

Our textbook—the Bible.

The study which we shall now bring you is Number 40 in our present series, entitled "Foundations".*

In this series of studies we are systematically examining the six doctrines which are listed in Hebrews chapter 6, verses 1 and 2, and which are there called "the beginning, or the foundation, of the doctrine of Christ". The six doctrines there listed are as follows: Number 1, "repentance from dead works"; Number 2, "faith toward God"; Number 3, "the doctrine of baptisms"; Number 4, "laying on of hands"; Number 5, "resurrection of the dead"; Number 6, "eternal judgment".

In our previous study we concluded our examination of the fourth of these foundation doctrines -- that which is called "laying on of hands". It therefore now remains for us to examine the last two doctrines in the list: Number 5, "resurrection of the dead"; and Number 6, "eternal judgment".

The examination of these last two doctrines leads us on into an altogether new realm of study. Hitherto, the four doctrines which we have considered have all been directly related to this present world and to the scene of time. However, in the study of the two doctrines now remaining, we are taken by the revelation of God's Word out of this present world and beyond the scene of time into a new realm—the realm of eternity. The scenes upon which will be enacted the resurrection of the dead and eternal judgment belong not to time, but to eternity.

Many people are confused by this word "eternity". They commonly tend to think of eternity as being merely an im-

*The first 39 studies in this series are published as five successive books, under the titles: "FOUNDATION FOR FAITH"; "REPENT AND BELIEVE"; "FROM JORDAN TO PENTECOST"; "PURPOSES OF PENTECOST"; "LAYING ON OF HANDS". See back cover of this book.

mensely long period of time, beyond the power of the human mind to conceive. However, this is not correct. Eternity is not merely the endless extension of time. Eternity differs in its nature from time. Eternity is an altogether different realm, a different mode of being. Eternity is God's own mode of being, the realm in which God Himself dwells.

In Genesis chapter 21, verse 33, and in Isaiah chapter 40, verse 28, God is called "the **everlasting** God".

In Psalm 90, verse 2, Moses addresses God, and says: "Before the mountains were brought forth, or ever thou hadst formed the earth and the world, even **from everlasting to everlasting,** thou art God."

In Isaiah chapter 57, verse 15, God Himself defines His own eternal nature and realm: "For thus saith the high and lofty One that **inhabiteth eternity,** whose name is Holy; I dwell in the high and holy place . . . "

These scriptures reveal that eternity is an aspect of God's own nature, the realm in which God has His being.

In the Old Testament the special, personal name of the one true God is revealed as "Jehovah". In the accepted Hebrew form, this name contains within it the basic elements of all the three main tense forms of the verb "to be"—future, present, and past. For this reason, in some modern versions, this name "Jehovah" is rendered "the Eternal". The true God is the One in whom past, present and future are all combined.

In Exodus chapter 3, verses 13 and 14, we read that Moses asked God by what name He wished to make Himself known to the children of Israel, and God gave Moses the following reply: "And God said unto Moses, I AM THAT I AM: and he said, Thus shalt thou say unto the children of Israel, I AM hath sent me unto you."

Here God gives Moses two forms of His name: "I AM", and "I AM THAT I AM". This reveals the eternal and unchanging nature of God. God is always "I AM". He is not in any way changed or affected by the course of time, which is but a part of His own creation. For God, past, present and future are ever united in an eternal present—an eternal "I AM".

In the New Testament, the same truths concerning the eternal, unchanging nature of God are brought out in the revelation granted to the apostle John upon the isle of

Patmos, as recorded in Revelation chapter 1, verse 8: "I am Alpha and Omega, the beginning, and the ending, saith the Lord, which is, and which was, and which is to come, the Almighty."

Alpha is the first letter of the Greek alphabet, and Omega the last. Thus, the whole alphabet of time, from its beginning to its ending, is contained within the nature of God Himself. The phrase, "which is, and which was, and which is to come," sums up present, past and future, and thus exactly corresponds to the revelation of God's nature contained in the Hebrew name, "Jehovah".

The other title of God here used, "the Almighty", corresponds to the Hebrew form used from the Book of Genesis onwards—"El Shaddai". For instance, in Genesis chapter 17, verse 1, we read that the Lord—that is, Jehovah—revealed Himself to Abraham by this name, "El Shaddai", "the Almighty God", for it says: "And when Abram was ninety years old and nine, the Lord appeared to Abram, and said unto him, I am the Almighty God (El Shaddai); walk before me, and be thou perfect."

The literal meaning of the form "El Shaddai" would appear to be "God who is sufficient"—that is, "the all-sufficient God"—the One in whom all creation is summed up, from its beginning to its ending.

The same picture of the absolute all-sufficiency of God is contained in the words of Paul in Romans chapter 11, verse 36: "For of him, and through him, and to him, are all things." All things have their origin in God; all things are kept in being by God; and all things find their end and their completion in God.

Thus, we find that the various Biblical names and titles of God contain within them a revelation of God's own eternal nature. And as we contemplate the eternal nature of God, thus revealed, we begin to form a true picture of eternity. Eternity, correctly understood, is not time in endless duration; rather, eternity is the nature and mode of God's own being, the uncreated realm in which God Himself exists.

Out of eternity, by the act, or process, of creation, God brought into being the present world, and, with it, the order of time as we now know it—past, present, and future. By another divine act, God will one day bring this present world to an end; and, with it, time, as we now know it, will once again cease to be. Time is directly and inseparably related to our present world order. With this world order time came into being, and with this world order time will once again cease to be.

Within the limits of this present world order, all creatures are subject to the processes of time. Time is one factor in man's total experience which he has no power to change. All men in this world are creatures and slaves of time. No man has the power to arrest the course of time, nor to reverse it.

This inexorable dominion of time in the affairs of men has always occupied the thoughts and imaginations of thinking men and women throughout the recorded history of the human race. In various different ways, and at various different periods, men have sought to escape from time's dominion—but always in vain. The English poet, Andrew Marvel, gave utterance to the cry of the human race when he said:

"Forever at my back I hear
Time's winged chariot drawing near."

In countless different forms and figures of speech, poets and philosophers from all ages and all backgrounds have given expression to the same thought—time's unalterable course and inexorable dominion over all men and all created things.

God Himself alone brought time into being, and God alone has power to arrest and to close the course of time. This is clearly stated in Revelation chapter 10, verses 5, 6, and 7:

"And the angel which I saw stand upon the sea and upon the earth lifted up his hand to heaven,

"And sware by him that liveth for ever and ever, who created heaven, and the things that therein are, and the earth, and the things that therein are, and the sea, and the things which are therein, that there should be time no longer:

"But in the days of the voice of the seventh angel, when he shall begin to sound, the mystery of God should be finished, as he hath declared to his servants the prophets."

Notice the simple, but tremendous authority of the angel's statement: "There shall be time no longer." Who but Almighty God could be responsible for such a declaration as that?

Indeed, we notice that the angel invokes the authority of God, first as the eternal One, and second as the Creator of all things, for it says that he (the angel) "lifted up his hand to heaven, and sware by him that **liveth for ever and ever,** who **created** heaven, and the things that therein are, and the earth, and the things that therein are, and the sea, and the things which are therein, that there should be time no longer . . . "

Thus, this statement concerning the end of time is based upon the authority of God Himself, first as the eternal One, "who liveth for ever and ever"; and second as the Creator, who brought all created things into being. This accords with the direct relationship which we have traced between the present world order and the course of time.

We notice also, in this passage from Revelation, that time is called a "mystery"; for it says, "the **mystery** of God shall be finished." In calling time a "mystery", the Bible is in perfect accord with the findings of philosophy and science. Time is indeed a "mystery", something that can never be fully understood or explained by man within the period of his present existence in this world.

In recent years the science of Physics, through the Theory of Relativity, has made a notable contribution to man's understanding of time. Briefly, this theory states that the two categories of time and space are inseparably related to each other, so that neither can be properly defined or explained, except in relation to the other. We cannot accurately define space without relation to time, nor time without relation to space. Together, these two constitute what science calls "the space-time continuum".

If we seek to relate this modern theory to the revelation of the Bible, we may say that this space-time continuum is the framework within which the whole of the present world order exists. By a sovereign act of God, this space-time continuum came into being together with the present world order; and by another sovereign act of God this present world order, together with the space-time continuum in which it exists, will once again cease to be. Before, behind and beyond the whole space-time continuum, the eternal nature and being of God continue unchanged.

The Bible reveals that, for the present world order as a whole, this, the end of time, will come at a moment preordained and known by God. However, there is a sense in which every individual even now alive must bow before this divine edict: "there shall be time no longer." As individuals, we do not necessarily need to wait for the end of the present world order. A moment lies ahead for each one of us when "time shall be no longer"—a moment when each one of us shall come to the end of time's course, and step out from time into eternity.

In the home of the late Chaim Waizmann, the first President of Israel, the hands of the clock now stand stationary at the hour of the President's death. This is a picture of that which awaits each man, no matter what may be his claim to fame or his station in life. For each man individually there comes an hour when the hands of the clock stand still—a moment when time ceases, and eternity begins.

Someone has expressed this same thought by saying: "the clock behind all other clocks is the human heart." When this clock ceases to beat, then all other clocks cease to tick. For each individual, the end of life is the end of time.

This is in line with the truth revealed in Leviticus chapter 17, verse 14: "For the life of all flesh is in the blood thereof." The Hebrew word here translated "life" is the word "nephesh". This word is more usually translated "soul". Thus, the Bible teaches that the soul—the invisible, immaterial, eternal element of man—is in some special way associated with the blood in his body. It is in the physical element of man's blood that the life and energy of his soul are effective.

This truth is illustrated in a remarkable way in the prophecy of Isaiah concerning Christ, in Isaiah chapter 53, verse 12: "Therefore will I divide him a portion with the great, and he shall divide the spoil with the strong; because he hath **poured out his soul unto death:** and he was numbered with the transgressors; and he bare the sin of many, and made intercession for the transgressors."

Here Isaiah prophetically reveals that at the time when Christ was to be numbered with the transgressors and to bear the sin of many, He would pour out his soul unto death. In fulfilment of this prophecy, the scriptures of the New Testament reveal that when Christ died upon the cross, every drop of His blood was poured forth from His body.

Thus, in pouring out His blood upon the cross, Christ poured out His very life—His soul—that that life might be accepted as a ransom, and a substitute, for sinners.

We may now apply this truth to the facts of physical death, as they affect the whole human race. The life—the soul—of each person is in the blood. As this invisible life of the soul is withdrawn from the physical body, the visible evidence is that the blood ceases to circulate in the blood vessels, and the heart ceases to beat. With the cessation of the heart's beating, death is normally said to have taken place. With the cessation of the heart's beating also, time ceases for the one concerned. At that moment the departing soul severs its contact with time, and steps out into eternity.

What awaits each departing soul as it steps from time into eternity? What is on the other side of time?

Doubtless there are many mysteries and things unknown that await each departing soul, concerning which the Bible does not lift the veil separating time from eternity. However, beyond the immediate threshold of eternity, there are two things which are clearly revealed by the Bible to be the ultimate destiny of all souls. These two things are: the resurrection of the dead, and eternal judgment.

The revelation that all men will be raised up again from the dead is clearly set forth by Paul in First Corinthians chapter 15, verse 22: "For as in Adam all die, even so in Christ shall all be made alive." Just as death is the universal fate of all, through their descent from Adam, so resurrection from the dead is the universal appointment of God for all; and this is made possible through the death and resurrection of Christ.

This is further explained by Paul in Romans chapter 14, verse 9: "For to this end Christ both died, and rose, and revived, that he might be Lord both of the dead and living." Paul here states two consequences of Christ's death and resurrection. First, Christ has thus become the Lord of both the dead and the living; His authority and power extend over all, both dead and living. Second, through this authority and power, Christ is able to revive all—that is, to resurrect all, to bring all back from the dead.

To this universal appointment of resurrection from the dead, the Bible admits only one class of exceptions; and the exception made in this case is a wholly logical one. Those who never die will never need to be resurrected from the dead. This is stated by Paul in First Corinthians chapter 15, verses 51 through 53:

"Behold, I shew you a mystery; We shall not all sleep, but we shall all be changed,

"In a moment, in the twinkling of an eye, at the last trump: for the trumpet shall sound, and the dead shall be raised incorruptible, and we shall be changed.

"For this corruptible must put on incorruption, and this mortal must put on immortality."

When Paul says here, "We shall not all sleep," he is referring only to true Christians, and he mans that all true Christians, who are alive at the time of Christ's return for His church, will not sleep—that is, will not die, will not sleep in death. Instead, their bodies will be instantaneously and miraculously changed, and they will find themselves arrayed in bodies of an entirely new and supernatural kind. Corruption will be replaced by incorruption, mortality by immortality. Thereafter there will remain no further possibility either of death or of resurrection from the dead.

Besides this class of true Christians who will be alive at the time of Christ's return, we may leave open the possibility of two other exceptions to the universal appointment of resurrection from the dead. These two other possible exceptions are provided by Enoch and Elijah, the two men recorded in the Old Testament who were translated from earth to heaven, without seeing death. The Bible nowhere gives clear or certain details as to what will be the ultimate experience of these two men. But one thing remains certain: those who never die will never need to be resurrected from the dead. On the other hand, the Bible does clearly reveal that all who do die will also be resurrected from the dead.

The other great appointment of God in eternity for all men is judgment.

That the world as a whole will have to face the judgment of God is clearly stated in Acts chapter 17, verses 30 and 31:

"And the times of this ignorance God winked at; but now commandeth all men everywhere to repent:

"Because he hath appointed a day, in the which he will judge the world in righteousness by that man whom he hath ordained; whereof he hath given assurance unto all men, in that he hath raised him from the dead."

Here Paul, who is the speaker in this passage, says definitely that God's appointment of judgment is made with the world at large, with the whole human race. It is for this reason that all men are now commanded to repent, because all men will one day be judged.

That Christians, too, must be prepared to stand before God's judgment is clearly stated by Paul in Romans chapter 14, verses 10 through 12:

"But why dost thou judge thy brother? or why dost thou set at nought thy brother? for we shall all stand before the judgment seat of Chrsit.

"For it is written, As I live, saith the Lord, every knee shall bow to me, and every tongue shall confess to God.

"So then every one of us shall give account of himself to God."

Here Paul is writing to Christians. Therefore, the phrase "thy brother" denotes a fellow Christian. Similarly, the phrase "every one of us" denotes every individual Christian. Furthermore, that there are no exceptions to judgment is indicated by the universal application of the two phrases, **"every knee shall bow . . . "** and **"every tongue shall confess to God."**

Later in this series of studies we shall go on to examine in detail God's program of judgment for all men, and we shall then see that there will be different scenes and purposes of judgment according to the various different categories of men to be judged. Meanwhile, this basic principle has been established, that all who die will be both resurrected and judged.

This principle itself is briefly and clearly stated in Hebrews chapter 9, verse 27: "It is appointed unto men once to die, but after this the judgment." Here the phrase, "it is appointed unto men," includes the whole human race generally.

We may say therefore that for every human soul who, through death, passes out of time into eternity, there remain two universal, irrevocable appointments of God: resurrection, and judgment.

Even those Christians who, through rapture at Christ's return, will escape death, must still appear before the judgment appointed for all Christians. For Paul says, in Romans chapter 14, verse 10: "We shall all stand before the judgment seat of Christ." Almost exactly the same words occur again in Second Corinthians chapter 5, verse 10: "We must all appear before the judgment seat of Christ." In each of these two passages, the phrase "we all" denotes all Christians, without any exceptions.

We may close this study by briefly pointing out one further principle, revealed in God's Word, which connects resurrection from the dead with eternal judgment. In every case, resurrection precedes judgment. In no case will man appear before God for judgment as a disembodied soul; but in every case it will be the complete man—the complete human personality, consisting of spirit, soul and body—that will appear before the judgment of God. For this reason, the resurrection of the body must necessarily precede the final judgment; and it is in this order that these two things are always presented to us in scripture: first, resurrection; then, eternal judgment.

The principle behind this is indicated in the words of Paul in Second Corinthians, chapter 5, verse 10 (the latter part of the verse): "For we must all appear before the judgment seat of Christ; that every one may receive **the things done in his body,** according to that he hath done, whether it be good or bad."

Notice that phrase, "the things done **in his body**". Judgment concerns the things done by man in his body while on earth. Since it is for the things done in the body that man must answer, therefore God has ordained that man shall appear in his body before God to answer for those things. Therefore resurrection of the body must precede eternal judgment. In this, as in all points, the program of God is logical and consistent.

*   *   *

In our next study, we shall begin to consider in detail what the Bible teaches about the resurrection of the body.

II
Diverging Destinies At Death

Man's Spirit Separated From His Body—The Righteous Separated From The Wicked

Welcome to the Study Hour.

Our textbook - the Bible.

The study which we shall now bring you is Number 41 in our present series, entitled "Foundations".

In this series of studies we are systematically examining the six doctrines which are listed in Hebrews chapter 6, verses 1 and 2, and which are there called "the beginning, or the foundation, of the doctrine of Christ". The six doctrines there listed are as follows: Number 1, "repentance from dead works"; Number 2, "faith toward God"; Number 3, "the doctrine of baptisms"; Number 4, "laying on of hands"; Number 5, "resurrection of the dead"; Number 6, "eternal judgment".

In our previous study we began to consider in a general way the last two doctrines in this list - that is, "resurrection of the dead", and "eternal judgment". We pointed out that there is an important difference between these two doctrines and the first four doctrines in the list, which we had already examined in our earlier studies. The first four doctrines are all directly related to this present world and to the scene of time; but the study of the last two doctrines leads us on beyond this present world and the scene of time, into the realm of eternity. We saw that, for every soul that, through death, steps out of time into eternity, there remain thereafter two universal and irrevocable appointments of almighty God: first, resurrection from the dead; and second, eternal judgment.

In our present study we shall now begin to examine in detail what the Bible teaches about the resurrection of the dead.

The first point which must be clearly established is that the part of man which is to be resurrected is his body—not his spirit, or his soul. Thus, more precisely defined, the resurrection of which the Bible speaks is a **resurrection of the body.** In order to understand this more clearly, it is necessary to analyse briefly the total nature of man, as revealed in the Bible.

In First Thessalonians chapter 5, verse 23, Paul gives expression to the following prayer on behalf of the Christians in Thessalonica: "And the very God of peace **sanctify you wholly;** and I pray God your **whole spirit and soul and body** be preserved blameless unto the coming of our Lord Jesus Christ."

In the first part of this verse Paul uses the phrase, "sanctify you **wholly**". This indicates that he is concerned with the total nature, or personality, of each of the Christians for whom he prays. In the second part of the verse Paul enumerates the three elements which together make up the total nature, or personality, of man. These three elements are: spirit, soul, and body.

Again, in Hebrews chapter 4, verse 12, we read: "For the word of God is quick, and powerful, and sharper than any two-edged sword, piercing even to the dividing asunder of soul and spirit, and of the joints and the marrow. . . "

This verse gives the same threefold division of man's total personality into spirit, soul and body—the body in this instance being represented by the actual physical parts here mentioned—that is, the joints and the marrow.

For a further revelation concerning the constitution of man's total personality we may turn to the original account of the creation of man, as given at the beginning of the Bible.

In Genesis chapter 1, verse 26, we read: "And God said, Let us make man in our image, after our likeness . . . "

In this verse two words are used to express the relationship of man, the creature, to God, the Creator. The first of these words is "image"; the second is "likeness".

The original Hebrew word, here translated "image", is, in many other passages of the Old Testament, translated by "shade" or "shadow". In modern Hebrew, the same root occurs today in the verbal form which means "to have one's photo taken". These associations of the word elsewhere in Hebrew indicate that its primary reference here, in the creation of man, is to man's external form, or appearance. Even in man's external form, there is a correspondence between man and God which is not found in the lower animal creation.

However, the correspondence between man and God goes further than mere external form. The second Hebrew word used here, and translated "likeness", is much more general in its application. It refers to the total personality of man. It indicates that there is a correspondence between this total personality of man and the being, or nature, of God Himself.

One important aspect of this correspondence between the nature of God and the nature of man is contained in the revelation of the three elements of man's total personality—spirit, soul and body. Thus we may say that man is revealed as a **triune** being—one total personality, yet composed of the **three** constituent elements—spirit, soul and body.

In a corresponding way, the Bible also reveals that the being of God Himself is **triune**—that is, there is **one** true God, yet within this **one** Godhead we discern the **three** distinct persons of the Father, the Son, and the Spirit.

Thus the Bible presents us with a likeness, or a correspondence, between the total personality of man and the total revelation of God's own nature. Briefly, we may sum up this correspondence of man to God, as follows: the Bible reveals a **triune** man, created in the likeness of a **triune** God.

In Genesis chapter 2, verse 7, we are given further facts concerning the original creation of man: "And the Lord God formed man of the dust of the ground, and breathed into his nostrils the breath of life; and man became a living soul."

Here we see that the total personality of man has its origin in two absolutely distinct and separate sources. The physical, material part of man—his body—is formed out of the dust of the earth. The invisible, immaterial part of man has its origin in the breath of almighty God. This invisible, immaterial part of man is here called "the soul". However, as we have already said, in other passages of scripture it is more fully defined as the combination of spirit and soul together. The Bible indicates that spirit and soul are not identical, but are two distinct elements together making up the immaterial part of man. However, it is outside the scope of our present study to attempt to draw a precise line of demarcation between man's spirit and his soul.

For our present purposes it is sufficient to say that the total personality of man has two different original sources.

The physical, material part of man—his body—is from below—from the earth. The invisible, immaterial part of man—his spirit and soul—is from above—from God Himself.

At death, the invisible, immaterial element of man—his spirit and soul—is released from its earthen vessel. Thereafter, by the process of burial, man's material part—his body—is restored again to the earth from which it came, and by the process of decomposition it returns again to its original elements. Even where there is no actual process of burial, man's body, after death, is always subjected to some process of disintegration or decomposition, which ultimately restores it to its original material elements.

Thus, it is man's **body** which, after death, is returned again to the material elements from which it was originally taken. Consequently, it will be man's **body** also which, by resurrection, will be raised up again from the same material elements.

There is no suggestion anywhere in the Bible that, after death, man's immaterial part—his spirit and soul—will be subjected to the same processes of burial and decomposition that await his body. On the contrary, there is evidence, in many different passages of scripture, that the destiny of man's spiritual part, after death, is quite different from that of his body.

For the first passage indicating that there is a difference in the destiny of the material and the spiritual parts of man, after death, we may turn to the Book of Ecclesiastes. In considering the teaching of this Book of Ecclesiastes, it is necessary to bear in mind a definite limitation which the author, Solomon, sets to all the enquiries and conclusions contained in the book.

This limitation is clearly indicated by one particular phase that is repeated again and again throughout the book. In Ecclesiastes chapter 1, verse 3, Solomon asks: "What profit hath a man of all his labour which he taketh **under the sun?**"

This same question, with slight variations in the wording, occurs altogether seven times throughout the book. Furthermore, the phrase "under the sun" occurs in other sentences in the book a further twenty times. In all, this particular phrase, "under the sun", occurs twenty-seven times in the book.

Thus, this phrase, "under the sun", indicates the deliberate limitation which Solomon sets to all his enquiries and conclusions in the book. The whole book throughout is concerned only with "things under the sun"—that is, with things which are subject to the sun's influence—things which are temporal and material—things which belong to the scene of time and to this present world order.

We may better understand this particular limitation by reference to the words of Paul in Second Corinthians chapter 4, verse 18, where he says: "For the things which are seen are temporal; but the things which are not seen are eternal." Here Paul draws a clear dividing line between two different classes of things: on the one hand, the things which are seen, and which are temporal; and on the other hand, the things which are unseen, and which are eternal.

If we now apply this twofold classification to the Book of Ecclesiastes, we find that the whole material contained within the book falls within the first class of things—those things which are seen and which are temporal. In this book, Solomon never seeks to pursue his studies beyond the boundary of the temporal realm, into the eternal realm. Wherever in his studies he reaches this boundary, he stops, and turns back to some new aspect of the temporal realm. This is indicated by the phrase which he uses twenty-seven times—"under the sun". There is nothing in the book that deals with the realm that is not subject to the sun's influence—the invisible and eternal realm. However, this invisible and eternal realm, which Solomon here leaves on one side, is referred to in various ways by nearly all the other books and authors of the Bible.

The realisation of this particular limitation of the Book of Ecclesiastes helps us better to appreciate the teaching of the book as a whole, and also clears up various apparent conflicts between the conclusions of Ecclesiastes and the teaching of other books of the Bible.

With this in mind, we may turn to the particular passage in Ecclesiastes which indicates a difference between the destiny of man's body at death, and that of his spirit. This is found in Ecclesiastes chapter 3, verses 18 through 21:

"I said in mine heart concerning the estate of the sons of men, that God might manifest them, and that they might see that they themselves are beasts.

"For that which befalleth the sons of men befalleth beasts; even one thing befalleth them: as the one dieth, so dieth the other; yea, they have all one breath; so that a man hath no preeminence over a beast: for all is vanity.

"All go unto one place; all are of the dust, and all turn to dust again.

"Who knoweth the spirit of man that goeth upward, and the spirit of the beast that goeth downward to the earth?"

In accordance with the whole theme of this book, Solomon lays his main emphasis upon the physical, material part of man—his body. Quite correctly, therefore, he points out that, in this respect, there is no difference between the destiny at death of man and of the lower animals. At death, the body of man, just like that of any other animal, is returned to the earth from which it came, and there decomposes once again into its component elements.

However, Solomon goes on to point out that this similarity between the destiny at death of man and of the lower animals ends with the physical body. It does not apply to man's spirit. Man's spirit—his immaterial part—has a different destiny from the spirit of the lower animals. This is indicated by the words of verse 21: "the spirit of man . . . goeth upward, and the spirit of the beast . . . goeth downward to the earth . . . "

Solomon introduces this verse with a question, "Who knoweth?" This is as if he were to say: "We recognise that there is a difference at this point between man and the beasts, but it is outside the scope of our present studies. Therefore, we can only mention it briefly; we cannot pursue it any further."

What are we to understand by the phrase which Solomon here uses concerning the spirit of man at the death of the body? He says: "the spirit of man . . . goeth upward."

First of all, we note that this is in accord with the account of man, as given in Genesis chapter 2, verse 7, which shows that man's body came from below, from the earth, but that his spirit came from above, from God. Because at death man's spirit is released from the body, the direction of his spirit is once again upward—towards God.

In Ecclesiastes chapter 12, verse 7, Solomon himself again returns to the theme of death, and he says: "Then shall the dust return to the earth as it was: and the spirit shall return unto God who gave it."

Thus, the teaching of Solomon in Ecclesiastes concerning the destiny of man's spirit at death is brief, but clear, and agrees with indications given in many other passages of scripture. At death, man's body returns to the dust, but the destiny of his spirit is upward, towards God.

What takes place when the spirit of man, at death, is released from the body, and is brought before God, the Creator?

There appears to be no definite revelation of scripture concerning this point. However, scripture does enable us to establish two definite principles in this connection. First, this appearance of the spirit of man before God is not for the purpose of the final judgment, which will take place only after the resurrection. Second, the spirits of the wicked and the ungodly can have no permanent access to the presence of God.

We may therefore conclude that this appearance of the spirit of man before God, immediately after death, is for one main purpose: to hear the divine sentence appointing to each spirit the state and the place which it must occupy from the time of death up to the time of resurrection and final judgment. Thereafter, each spirit is consigned to its duly appointed state and place, and continues there until called forth again at the resurrection of the body.

What is the condition of departed spirits in this period that intervenes between death and resurrection?

Doubtless there is much concerning this that God has not seen fit to reveal in the Bible. However, there are two facts which certainly are made clear in the Bible. The first fact is that, after death, there is a complete and permanent separation between the departed spirits of the righteous and those of the wicked. The second fact is that the condition of the departed spirits of the righteous was different in the period before the death and resurrection of Christ from their condition now, in this present dispensation.

Over and above these two clearly established facts, the Bible does from time to time lift a corner of the veil between this world and the next, thus giving us a momentary glimpse of that which lies beyond.

For example, in Isaiah chapter 14, verses 9 and 10, we are given a picture of God's judgment upon the oppressing king of Babylon:

"Hell—that is, sheol—from beneath is moved for thee to meet thee at thy coming: it stirreth up the dead for thee, even all the chief ones of the earth; it hath raised up from their thrones all the kings of the nations.

"All they shall speak and say unto thee, Art thou also become weak as we? art thou become like unto us?"

This account reveals certain definite facts about the condition of departed spirits. It does not suggest that there is any knowledge of events currently transpiring on earth; nor necessarily any recollection of events that have transpired during the earthly lifetime of these departed spirits. On the other hand, it does clearly indicate that there is a definite persistence of personality after death; there is recognition of one person by another; there is communication between one person and another; and there is an awareness of present conditions in this place of departed spirits. Furthermore, there is a correspondence in some measure between a man's state in this world and his state in the next. For those who were kings in this world are still recognised as kings in the next.

In Ezekiel chapter 32, verses 17 through 32, we are given a somewhat similar picture of the descent into sheol of the departed spirit of the king of Egypt.

In verses 18 and 19 of this chapter, God speaks to Ezekiel as follows:

"Son of man, wail for the multitude of Egypt, and cast them down, even her, and the daughters of the famous nations, unto the nether parts of the earth, with them that go down into the pit.

"Whom dost thou pass in beauty? go down, and be thou laid with the uncircumcised."

Then in verse 21 we are told of the reception accorded to the king of Egypt by the spirits of other great men that have gone down into the pit before him: "The strong among the mighty shall speak to him out of the midst of hell with them that help him: they are gone down, they lie uncircumcised, slain by the sword."

A careful examination of this passage will show that it reproduces the same features already noted in the passage from Isaiah, previously examined. There is persistence of personality; there is recognition of one person by another; there is communication between one person and another;

there is awareness of present conditions in this place of departed spirits.

Let us now turn on to the New Testament and see what further light this sheds upon the destiny of man's spiritual part at death.

The first New Testament passage that we shall consider is the well-known story of the beggar, Lazarus, who was laid daily at the rich man's gate. This is found in Luke chapter 16, verses 19 through 31. There is no suggestion that this story is a mere parable. It is related by Christ Himself as an actual historical incident that had taken place at some time prior to that point in Christ's earthly ministry—that is, in the dispensational period prior to Christ's death and resurrection.

The actual passage dealing with the destiny of Lazarus and the rich man after death is contained in verses 22 through 26:

"And it came to pass, that the beggar died, and was carried by the angels into Abraham's bosom: the rich man also died, and was buried;

"And in hell he lifted up his eyes, being in torments, and seeth Abraham afar off, and Lazarus in his bosom.

"And he cried and said, Father Abraham, have mercy on me, and send Lazarus, that he may dip the tip of his finger in water, and cool my tongue; for I am tormented in this flame.

"But Abraham said, Son, remember that thou in thy lifetime receivedst thy good things, and likewise Lazarus evil things; but now he is comforted, and thou art tormented.

"And beside all this, between us and you there is a great gulf fixed: so that they which would pass from hence to you cannot; neither can they pass to us, that would come from thence."

There is much in this passage that confirms the conclusions that we had already formed from the Old Testament. At death, the body by burial is returned to the earth, but the spirit moves out into a new kind of existence. In this existence after death, there is persistence of personality; there is recognition of one person by another; there is consciousness of present conditions. All this agrees with the picture given in the Old Testament.

However, this passage in Luke adds one further, very important fact. After death, the destiny of the spirits of the righteous is quite different from that of the spirits of the wicked. Both Lazarus and the rich man found themselves within the realm of departed spirits, called in Hebrew "sheol" and in Greek "hades"; but their destinies there were quite different. The rich man's spirit was in a place of torment; the spirit of Lazarus was in a place of rest. Between these two places there was fixed an impassable gulf, that could not be crossed from either side.

The place of rest, set apart for the departed spirits of the righteous, is here called "Abraham's bosom". This title would indicate that this place is ordained for the spirits of all those who in their earthly pilgrimage followed in the footsteps of faith and obedience marked out by Abraham, who for this reason is called "the father of all them that believe".

*　　　*　　　*

In our next study we shall consider further passages in the New Testament dealing with the destiny of man's spirit after death; and we shall seek to relate this whole subject to the doctrine of the resurrection.

III

Christ The Pattern And The Proof

*His Experiences Between Death And Resurrection—Destiny
Of The Christian At Death—Resurrection Restores The Same
Body That Died*

Welcome to the Study Hour.

Our textbook - the Bible.

The study which we shall now bring you is Number 42 in our present series, entitled "Foundations".

In our last study we began to examine in detail that doctrine of the Christian faith which is called in Hebrews chapter 6, verse 2, "resurrection of the dead".

In order to understand clearly what the Bible teaches about the resurrection of the dead, we were led to consider briefly the total nature, or personality, of man. We saw that the Bible reveals a triune man, created in the likeness of a triune God. That is, man consists of three elements, which together make up his complete personality. These three elements are revealed as the spirit, the soul, and the body. Of these, the body is the material part of man; the spirit and soul together make up the immaterial part of man. Man's material part, his body, has its origin in the dust of the earth; man's immaterial part, his spirit and soul, has its origin in the breath, or spirit, of almighty God.

At death, the body, by some process of disintegration or decomposition, returns to its original material elements; while the spirit passes out into a new realm of being. Prior to the time of Christ's death and resurrection, this realm, into which the departed spirits of men passed, was called by the Hebrew name "sheol", and by the Greek name "hades". These two names are normally translated in the King James version by the English word "hell".

The particular state or location of each departed spirit in "sheol", or "hades", was decided by the sentence of almighty God, according to the life that each had led while on earth. There was a complete and impassable gulf of separation between the departed spirits of the righteous and those of the wicked. The spirits of the righteous were consigned to a place of rest, called in one passage "Abraham's bosom". The spirits of the wicked were consigned to a place of torment.

Hitherto, we have gleaned these facts concerning the destiny of departed spirits from passages of scripture which all deal with events that transpired prior to the death and resurrection of Christ. We shall now go on to consider what the Bible reveals about the experience of Christ Himself during the period between His death and His resurrection.

The first passage which we shall consider is a prophetic anticipation of the death, burial and resurrection of Christ, contained in the words of Psalm 16, verses 8 through 11:

"I have set the Lord always before me: because he is at my right hand, I shall not be moved.

"Therefore my heart is glad, and my glory rejoiceth: my flesh also shall rest in hope.

"For thou wilt not leave my soul in hell (that is, "sheol"); neither wilt thou suffer thine Holy One to see corruption.

"Thou wilt show me the path of life: in thy presence is fulness of joy; at thy right hand are pleasures for evermore."

In Acts chapter 2, verses 25 through 28, Peter quotes these verses in full. In Acts chapter 13, verse 35, Paul quotes one of these verses. Both Peter and Paul alike interpret these words as a direct prophecy of the burial and resurrection of Christ. Peter points out that, though these words were spoken by David, they do not apply to David, because David's soul was left for many centuries in "sheol" and his body suffered the process of corruption. Therefore this is one of many Messianic prophecies in the Old Testament, spoken by David, yet referring not to David himself, but to David's promised seed, the Messiah, Jesus Christ.

Applied in this way to Christ, these words of David in Psalm 16 reveal two things that transpired at the death of Christ. First, His body was laid in the tomb, but did not suffer any process of corruption. Second, His spirit descended into "sheol" (the place of departed spirits), but did not remain there for longer than the period between His death and His resurrection.

This Old Testament revelation is confirmed by the more detailed revelation of the New Testament.

In Luke chapter 23, verse 43, we read that Jesus said to the penitent thief beside Him on the cross: "Today shalt thou be with me in paradise." (The word "paradise" means literally "a garden", and is one of the names given to that place in the next world which is reserved for the departed spirits of the righteous).

Again in Luke chapter 23, verse 46, we read: "And when Jesus had cried with a loud voice, he said, Father, into thy hands I commend my spirit: and having said thus, he gave up the ghost"—or, in more modern English, "he expired."

By the words, "Father, into thy hands I commend my spirit," we understand that Jesus here committed the destiny of His spirit at death into the hands of His heavenly Father. His body, He knew, was to be laid aside in the tomb; but the destiny of His spirit was to be decided by God, His Father.

In all this we see that Jesus, having taken upon Himself, in addition to His divine nature, the nature of humanity, passed through the same experiences that await each human soul at death. His body was committed to the tomb, in burial, by the hands of men; but His spirit was committed into the hands of God, and its destiny was settled by the sentence of God.

What happened to the spirit of Christ, after it was thus released, at death, from the earthen vessel of His body?

In Ephesians chapter 4, verses 9 and 10, we read, concerning Christ: "Now that he ascended, what is it but that he also descended first into the lower parts of the earth?

"He that descended is the same also that ascended up far above all heavens, that he might fill all things."

Again, in First Peter chapter 3, verses 18 through 20, we read:

"For Christ also hath once suffered for sins, the just for the unjust, that he might bring us to God, being put to death in the flesh, but quickened by the spirit:

"By which also he went and preached unto the spirits in prison;

"Which sometime were disobedient, when once the long-suffering of God waited in the days of Noah . . . "

If we combine the various revelations contained in these passages of scripture concerning Christ, we may form the following outline of the experiences through which the spirit of Christ passed.

His spirit descended into "sheol", the place of departed spirits. On the day of His death upon the cross, He went first to the place of the spirits of the righteous, called "paradise", or "Abraham's bosom". Since the gospel record indicates that the death of Christ on the cross preceded the death of the two thieves, it seems natural to suppose that Christ Himself was in paradise to welcome the departed spirit of the penitent thief, who followed him there.

From "paradise" Christ then went on further down into that area of "sheol" reserved for the spirits of the wicked. It would appear that His descent into this place of torment was necessary for Him to complete the work of atonement for man's sin, since He had to endure in full not merely the physical, but also the spiritual consequences of sin.

At some stage while in this lower realm of "sheol", Christ preached to the spirits of those who had lived wickedly in the days of Noah (that is, the antediluvian age), and who had consequently been consigned to a special place of imprisonment in "sheol". (The Greek verb here translated "preached" is directly connected with the Greek noun "herald". It does not therefore necessarily indicate that Christ "preached the gospel" to these spirits in prison; but merely that He made to them some "proclamation", such as a herald would make.)

Then, at God's appointed moment, when all the divine purposes of the atonement had been accomplished, the spirit of Christ ascended up again from the realm of "sheol" to the realm of this present temporal world. At the same time, His body, which had been lying lifeless in the tomb, was raised up from death; and spirit and body were once again reunited to form a complete personality.

Concerning Christ's resurrection, Paul says in First Corinthians chapter 15, verses 20 and 22:

"But now is Christ risen from the dead, and become the firstfruits of them that slept . . .

"For as in Adam all die, even so in Christ shall all be made alive."

By these words Paul indicates that the resurrection of Christ from the dead sets a pattern which is to be followed by all men. In this pattern we may distinguish two main parts. First, man's immaterial part—his spirit—is to come forth once again from the realm of departed spirits. Second, his material part—his body—is to be raised up again from death. In this way, spirit and body are once again to be reunited, thus reconstituting the complete personality of man, with its material and immaterial parts—its three elements of spirit, soul and body.

*   *   *

In order to complete our brief outline of this subject, it is necessary to carry our study beyond the time of Christ's own death and resurrection, and to consider what the New Testament reveals concerning the destiny at death of true believing Christians in this present dispensation. We shall see that the New Testament indicates one important difference in this respect between the period that preceded Christ's resurrection, and that which followed it.

As we have already seen, prior to Christ's resurrection, the departed spirits of the righteous were consigned to a certain area of "sheol", the nether world, which was called "paradise", or "Abraham's bosom". However, it is very plain that once full atonement for sin had actually been accomplished by the death and resurrection of Christ, thereafter the way was open for the spirits of the righteous to ascend immediately and directly into heaven and into the very realm and presence of God Himself.

This is made plain by a number of passages in the New Testament.

For example, in Acts chapter 7, we read the account of the stoning of Stephen, the first Christian martyr.

In Acts chapter 7, verses 55 and 56, the account reads as follows:

"But he (Stephen), being full of the Holy Ghost, looked up stedfastly into heaven, and saw the glory of God, and Jesus standing on the right hand of God,

"And said, Behold, I see the heavens opened, and the Son of man standing on the right hand of God."

Then, in verses 59 and 60, the account closes as follows:

"And they stoned Stephen, calling upon God, and saying, Lord Jesus, receive my spirit.

"And he kneeled down, and cried with a loud voice, Lord, lay not this sin to their charge. And when he had said this, he fell asleep."

From this account it is plain that in the moments just before death, Stephen was granted a vision of Christ in glory at the right hand of God. Thereafter, his prayer, "Lord Jesus, receive my spirit," indicated his assurance that immediately upon the death of his body, his spirit would ascend direct into heaven, into the presence of God.

This is confirmed by the way in which the apostle Paul also speaks about death.

In Second Corinthians chapter 5, verses 6 and 8, Paul says:

"Therefore we are always confident, knowing that, whilst we are at home in the body, we are absent from the Lord: . . .

"We are confident, I say, and willing rather to be absent from the body, and to be present with the Lord."

These words of Paul imply two things. First, while the spirit of the believer remains within his body, his spirit cannot be in the immediate presence of God. Second, as soon as the spirit of the believer is released by death from the body, it has direct access to the presence of God.

Paul returns to the same thought again in Philippians, where he weighs the relative merits of being released by death from his physical body, or of remaining longer in his body, in order to be able to fulfil his earthly ministry for Christ. In discussing these two alternatives, Paul says in Philippians chapter 1, verses 21 through 24:

"For to me to live is Christ, and to die is gain.

"But if I live in the flesh, this is the fruit of my labour: yet what I shall choose I wot not.

"For I am in a strait betweixt two, having a desire to depart, and to be with Christ; which is far better:

"Nevertheless to abide in the flesh is more needful for you."

Here Paul considers two alternatives before him: the first, "to abide in the flesh"—that is, to continue longer in his present life here on earth, in his physical body; the second, "to depart, and to be with Christ"—that is, for his spirit to be released from his body, by death, and thus to enter directly into the presence of Christ in heaven.

These examples of Stephen and Paul make it plain that, when a true Christian in this present dispensation dies, his spirit is thereby released from his body, and thereupon goes immediately and directly into the presence of Christ in heaven. This direct access for the Christian believer into the presence of God in heaven has been made possible only through the death and resurrection of Christ, by which full and final atonement has been made for sin. Prior to Christ's atonement, the departed spirits of the righteous were consigned to a special area in "sheol", the nether world. This special area was a place of rest and comfort, not of torment or punishment. Nevertheless, it was far removed from the immediate presence of God.

We may now apply the conclusions which we have reached to the doctrine of the resurrection. The pattern for the resurrection of all men is set by the resurrection of Christ Himself. That is to say, the departed spirit is called forth from the place to which it has been consigned by the sentence of God—whether in the realm of heaven or of the nether world. At the same time, the body is raised up by resurrection from death. Spirit and body are thus reunited, and the complete personality of man is reconstituted.

*   *   *

At this point, there is a difficulty that often troubles the carnal mind, concerning the resurrection of man's physical body. Suppose that a man has been dead two or three thousand years and that his body in this period of time has been totally resolved into its original material elements. Or suppose that, in more recent times, a man has been killed in war by the explosion of a bomb or a shell, and that his body has been totally disintegrated by the force of the explosion, so that no humanly recoverable traces of the body remain. It is reasonable, in such circumstances, to expect that, at the moment of resurrection, the material elements of bodies such as these shall be regathered, reconstituted, and resurrected complete once again?

The answer must be that, for those who acknowledge the unlimited wisdom, knowledge, and power of God, there is nothing incredible or impossible in this doctrine. Furthermore, when we take time to consider what the Bible reveals concerning the wisdom and knowledge of God displayed in the original creation of man's body, the doctrine of the resurrection of the body is made to appear both natural and logical.

The most detailed account of the original process by which God formed man's physical body is given by David in Psalm 139. Nearly the whole of this Psalm is devoted to extolling the fathomless wisdom, knowledge and power of God. In particular, in Psalm 139, verses 13 through 16, David deals with these attributes of God as displayed in the formation of his physical body, for he says:

"For thou hast possessed my reins: thou hast covered me in my mother's womb.

"I will praise thee; for I am fearfully and wonderfully made: marvellous are thy works; and that my soul knoweth right well.

"My substance—that is, my physical body—was not hid from thee; when I was made in secret, and curiously wrought in the lowest parts of the earth.

"Thine eyes did see my substance—my physical body—yet being unperfect; and in thy book all my members were written, which is continuance were fashioned, when as yet there was none of them."

Here David is speaking not about the immaterial part of his nature—his spirit and soul; but about the material part of his nature—his physical body—which he denotes by the phrases "my substance" and "my members".

Concerning the process by which God brought his physical body into being, David reveals two facts of great interest and importance.

The first fact is this: the material, earthly elements out of which David's body was to be formed were specially appointed and prepared a great while beforehand by God, while these material elements were still "in the lowest part of the earth".

The second fact is this: God had appointed the precise number, dimensions and material of all the constituent members of David's body, long before his body ever actually came into being; and as each one of these members thereafter came into being, God prepared and maintained a precise record of each of them.

Although at first sight this revelation might appear fanciful to some people, it is actually implied in the words of Jesus in Matthew chapter 10, verse 30: "But the very hairs of your head are all numbered." If God keeps a record of each individual hair on the human head, is there any other part of the human body which could be considered too small or two unimportant for God to keep both a number and a record of it?

In the light of this revelation, we find that there is a close and illuminating parallel between the original process by which God formed man's physical body, and the process by which He will once again resurrect that body from death.

In the original process of forming man's body, God first appointed and prepared the various material elements of that body, while they were still in the earth. Then, as these appointed elements were assembled together to constitute man's body, God kept a precise and careful record of each part and each member.

After death, the body decomposes once again into its material elements. But God, who foreordained the special elements of each individual body, still keeps a record of each element. Then, at the moment of resurrection, by His same creative power He once again reassembles every one of the original elements and thus reconstitutes the same body. The only major difference is that the original process of forming the body was apparently gradual, while the process of reconstituting the body at the resurrection will be instantaneous. However, in relation to God's supreme and sovereign control of both time and space, the actual length of time required is of no significance whatever.

If we do not accept this Biblical account of the destiny of man's body, then we have no right to speak of a "resurrection"—that is, of a process of raising again the second time. If the elements which make up man's body at resurrection are not the same as those which originally made up his body, then there is no logical or causal connection between the first and the second body. The two bodies are in no way related to each other, neither in time, nor in space. In that case, we should not be able to say that God resurrected, or raised up, man's body. We should have to say, instead, that God equipped man's spirit with a totally new body, unconnected in any way with the previous body. However, this is not what the Bible teaches. The Bible teaches that there is direct continuity between man's original body and the body with which he will be provided at the resurrection. The continuity consists in this: that the same material elements which formed the original body will once again be reassembled to form the resurrection body.

Confirmation of this wonderful truth is found first and foremost in resurrection of Christ Himself. When Jesus first appeared to His disciples in a group after His resurrection, they were frightened, supposing that what they saw was a ghost, a disembodied spirit. However, Jesus immediately reassured them, and gave them positive proof of His identity and of the reality of His body, for we read in Luke chapter 24, verses 39 and 40, that He said to them:

"Behold my hands and my feet, that is I myself: handle me, and see; for a spirit hath not flesh and bones, as ye see me have.

"And when he had thus spoken, he shewed them his hands and his feet."

It happened that one of the disciples, Thomas, was not present on this occasion, and he would not accept the account of the incident which the other disciples gave him. However, in John chapter 20, verse 27, we read that a week later Jesus appeared to the disciples again, when Thomas was also present, and this time He addressed Himself directly to Thomas:

"Then saith he to Thomas, Reach hither thy finger, and behold my hands; and reach hither thy hand, and thrust it into my side: and be not faithless, but believing."

From these passages we see that Jesus was careful to give His disciples the plainest evidence that, after His resurrection, He had a real body, and that his body was the same that had been crucified. The evidence of this was in His hands and feet and in His side, which still bore the marks of the nails and of the spear. In other respects His body had undergone certain important changes. It was no longer subject to the limitations of a mortal body in this present world order. Jesus could now appear or disappear at will; He could enter a closed room; He could pass between earth and heaven. However, with due allowance made for these changes, it was still in other respects the same body that had been crucified.

Furthermore, Jesus also promised His disciples that their bodies would be resurrected no less complete than His own.

In Luke chapter 21, Jesus first warned His disciples of great opposition and persecution awaiting them. In particular, He warned them that some of them would actually be put to death. Nevertheless, He went on to give them a clear promise of the resurrection of their bodies. This warning, and the promise that follows it, are found in Luke chapter 21, verses 16 through 18:

"And ye shall be betrayed both by parents, and brethren, and kinsfolks, and friends; and some of you shall they cause to be put to death.

"And ye shall be hated of all men for my name's sake.

"But there shall not an hair of your head perish."

Notice carefully what Jesus says here. The disciples shall be hated, persecuted, killed. Yet, at the end of it all, "not a hair of their head shall perish." This does not refer to the preservation of their physical bodies intact in this life. In many cases we know that the early Christians—as also those of later ages—suffered violent death, mutilation, burning, and other processes that marred and destroyed their physical bodies. Therefore the promise of every hair perfectly preserved does not refer to this present life, but to the resurrection of their bodies from the dead. At the resurrection, every element and member of their original physical bodies, foreordained, numbered, and recorded by God, will by God's omnipotence once again be regathered and reconstituted—a perfect body—a glorified body—but still the same body that had previously suffered death and decomposition.

Such is the picture that the Bible gives of the resurrection of man's body: wonderful in its revelation of God's unlimited wisdom, knowledge, and power; yet perfectly consistent with logic and with the principles of scripture.

* * *

In our next study we shall go on to consider the prophetic picture of the resurrection presented to us in the Old Testament.

IV
Resurrection Foretold
In The Old Testament

Prophecies Of The Psalms, Genesis, Job, Isaiah, Daniel, Hosea—Believers To Be Included In Christ's Resurrection

Welcome to the Study Hour.

Our textbook - the Bible.

The study which we shall now bring you is Number 43 in our present series, entitled "Foundations".

In our last two studies we have been examining in detail that doctrine of the Christian faith which is called, in Hebrews chapter 6, verse 2, "resurrection of the dead".

We may now briefly summarise the conclusions which we have so far reached.

The total personality of man consists of a material part, which is the body, and an immaterial part, which is made up of the spirit and the soul combined. At death, man's body, by some process of disintegration or decomposition, returns to its original material elements; while the spirit passes out into a new realm of being. Prior to the death and resurrection of Christ, this realm of departed spirits, both the righteous and the wicked, was in the lower world, called "sheol", or "hades". However, within this lower world, the place set apart for the spirits of the righteous was separated by an impassable gulf from the place set apart for the spirits of the wicked. Since the death and resurrection of Christ, the departed spirits of true Christians no longer descend into the lower world, but have direct access into the realm of God's presence in heaven.

At the moment of resurrection, the departed spirit is called forth from the place to which it has been consigned by the sentence of God—whether in the realm of heaven or of the lower world. At the same moment, the material elements of the body are raised up and reassembled. Spirit and body are thus reunited, and the complete personality of man is reconstituted.

In our present study we shall now go on to show that the divine promise of the resurrection runs as one continuous thread throughout the whole Bible, both Old and New Testament alike.

In First Corinthians chapter 15, verse 4, Paul makes the following statement concerning the burial and resurrection of Christ: "He (Christ) was buried, and rose again the third day **according to the scriptures.**"

We must bear in mind that at the period when Paul wrote these words, the only complete, acknowledged scriptures already in being were those of the Old Testament. Consequently, when Paul says here that Christ rose again the third day **according to the scriptures,** he means that the resurrection of Christ was a fulfilment of the scriptures of the Old Testament. Furthermore, Paul refers to the Old Testament scriptures as being the first, and basic, authority for the doctrine of the resurrection. Thereafter, he goes on to cite the evidence of men still alive at that time who had been eyewitnesses of the risen Christ. However, in Paul's presentation of this doctrine, this evidence of contemporary eyewitnesses is secondary to that of the Old Testament scriptures.

Let us therefore consider some of the main passages in the Old Testament which prophetically foreshow the resurrection.

In our previous studies on this subject we have already shown that there is a clear promise of the burial and resurrection of Christ in Psalm 16, verses 8 through 11. We pointed out that, although these verses were spoken in the first person by David, they do not actually apply to David himself, but rather to David's promised seed, the Messiah, Jesus Christ; and that they are applied in this way to Christ in the New Testament both by Peter and by Paul.

In Psalm 71, verses 20 and 21, there is another similar passage prophetically foreshowing the resurrection of Christ. David is here speaking directly to God, and he says:

"Thou, which hast shewed me great and sore troubles, shalt quicken me again, and shalt bring me up again from the depths of the earth.

"Thou shalt increase my greatness, and comfort me on every side."

This passage is another example of Messianic prophecy. That is to say, the words are spoken in the first person by

David; yet they do not apply primarily to David, but to David's promised seed, the Messiah, Jesus Christ.

Understood in this way, this passage prophetically sets forth five successive stages that Christ was to pass through in making atonement for man's sin. These five stages may be summarised as follows:

First, "great and sore troubles"—that is, the rejection, suffering, scourging and crucifixion of Christ.

Second, Christ was to descend into "the depths of the earth"—that is, into sheol, or hades, the place of departed spirits.

Third, Christ was to be "quickened"—that is, made alive again.

Fourth, Christ was to be "brought up again" from sheol—that is, the resurrection of Christ.

Fifth, after the resurrection of Christ, he was to be "made great and comforted"—that is, restored once again to His place of fellowship and supreme authority at the right hand of God His Father.

Time and space are not sufficient to quote the many passages in the New Testament which confirm that this prophecy was exactly and completely fulfilled in the experience of Christ.

However, the two Old Testament passages which we have so far examined, in Psalm 16 and Psalm 71, refer primarily to the resurrection of Christ Himself, as the Messiah. Let us now examine other passages of the Old Testament which foreshow the resurrection of others beside Christ Himself.

Let us begin by considering one of God's promises made to Abraham. This is found in Genesis chapter 17, verse 8. God is here speaking directly to Abraham, and he says: "And I will give unto thee, and to thy seed after thee, the land wherein thou art a stranger, all the land of Canaan, for an everlasting possession. . . ."

There are two important points to notice in this promise here made by God to Abraham concerning the possession of the land of Canaan.

First of all, the **order** of possession is important. God says: "unto thee, and to thy seed after thee." That is to say, Abraham himself is to possess the land first, and then his seed—his descendants—after him.

Second, the **extent** and **duration** of possession are important. God says: "**all** the land of Canaan, for an **everlasting** possession". This promise cannot be fulfilled by any occupation of the land that is partial or temporary. Its fulfilment demands a complete and permanent possession of the whole land.

It is plain therefore that up to now this promise of God to Abraham has never been fulfilled. The only part of the land that Abraham himself has hitherto received for a permanent possession is just space enough in which to be buried—that is, the burial place in the cave of Machpelah in the field of Ephron the Hittite, near Hebron.

As for Abraham's seed, the nation of Israel, up until now they have enjoyed temporary or partial occupation of the land, but they have never known the complete and permanent possession here promised by God. At present, the newly formed state of Israel clings tenaciously, in face of threats and opposition, to an area that is a small fraction of the total possession promised by God.

Even if, in the years that lie ahead, Israel should by one means or another extend their area of occupation, until they gain control of the whole land promised to them by God, this still would not constitute a complete fulfilment of God's original promise, for God's promise to Abraham was, "unto **thee,** and to thy seed **after thee**". That is to say, Abraham himself must first enjoy possession of the whole land, and then his seed—his descendants—after him.

Thus, this promise of God cannot be fulfilled apart from the resurrection. The cave of Machpelah must first give up its dead. Abraham himself must be resurrected. Only in this way can he ever enter into the full possession of the land in which he now lies buried. If there is no resurrection, then God's promise to Abraham can never be fulfilled. The promise of God here made to Abraham assumes, and depends upon, the resurrection. We find therefore that this promise to Abraham concerning the everlasting possession of the land of Canaan includes within it the promise of Abraham's own resurrection from the dead; and in this way the truth of the resurrection is already revealed in the book of Genesis, the first book of the Old Testament.

Let us now turn to another book of the Old Testament, which is usually attributed to an early date—that is, the book of Job. In the midst of overwhelming grief and affliction, when his earthly future appears to be without a single ray of hope, Job gives utterance to an amazing confession of faith concerning the eternal destiny of his soul and the resurrection of his body. This confession is found in Job chapter 19, verses 25 through 27:

"For I know that my redeemer liveth, and that he shall stand at the latter day upon the earth:

"And though after my skin worms destroy this body, yet in my flesh shall I see God:

"Whom I shall see for myself, and mine eyes shall behold and not another. . . "

The language of Job is so terse, and so charged with meaning, that it is difficult to find any one translation which adequately brings out the full force of the original. The following is an alternative translation of the central section of the passage just quoted:

"After I shall awake, though this body be destroyed, yet out of my flesh shall I see God . . . "

Whichever translation we may prefer, certain facts stand out with absolute clarity from this passage. Job knows that his physical body will suffer the process of decomposition. Nevertheless, he looks forward to a period at the end of time when he will again be clothed with a body of flesh, and when he will appear in that body directly before God. This assurance of Job is based on the life of one whom he calls "my redeemer". Thus the whole passage is a clear anticipation of the final resurrection of Job's body, made possible through the resurrection life of the Redeemer, Jesus Christ.

We may now turn on to the prophet Isaiah, who lived about seven hundred years before Christ. In Isaiah, chapter 26, verse 19, we find a confession of faith in the resurrection, somewhat similar to that of Job, which we have already considered. Isaiah says here: "Thy dead men shall live, together with my dead body shall they arise. Awake and sing, ye that dwell in dust: for thy dew is as the dew of herbs, and the earth shall cast out the dead."

Isaiah speaks here about his own dead body arising from the dust, and together with this he associates a group whom he calls, at the beginning of the verse, "thy dead men", and again, more generally, at the end of the verse, "the dead". It is plain that Isaiah contemplates here a general resurrection of many, if not all, of the dead. The prospect is one that brings joy to those concerned, for Isaiah says, "Awake, **and sing,** ye that dwell in dust." It would seem therefore that Isaiah's message is addressed primarily to the righteous dead, who, through the resurrection, will be ushered into their final, eternal reward.

In agreement with conclusions reached in earlier studies, we see that Isaiah veiws the resurrection as affecting primarily the material part of man—his body. He speaks about those "that dwell **in dust**". Thus the picture which he presents is that of men's dead bodies, arising, or awakening, out of their sleep in the dust.

This verse of Isaiah also contains a revelation as to the power which will effect the resurrection. Isaiah refers to this power under the figure of "**dew**", for he says: "Thy dew is as the dew of herbs, and the earth shall cast out the dead". The picture is one of dry seeds lying buried in the dust, and requiring moisture to make them germinate and spring up. This moisture is provided by the dew settling upon them. In many passages of scripture, "dew"—like rain—is a figure of the operation of the Holy Spirit. Thus Isaiah foreshows that the resurrection of the dead bodies of believers will be effected through the power of the Holy Spirit. This is in complete agreement with the words of Paul in Romans chapter 8, verse 11: "But if the Spirit of him that raised up Jesus from the dead dwell in you, he that raised up Christ from the dead shall also quicken—that is, make alive—your mortal bodies **by his Spirit** that dwelleth in you." Paul here states that the same power of the Holy Spirit, that raised the dead body of Jesus out of the tomb, will also raise up the dead bodies of those who believe in Jesus and who are indwelled by the Holy Spirit.

The next main Old Testament prophecy of the resurrection which we shall consider is found in Daniel chapter 12, verses 1 through 3. These verses are part of a lengthy prophetic revelation concerning the last days, given to Daniel by the angel Gabriel, who was sent to him by God for that special purpose. This part of the revelation, which deals specifically with the resurrection, is as follows:

"And at that time shall Michael stand up, the great prince which standeth for the children of thy people: and there shall be a time of trouble, such as never was since there was a nation even to that same time: and at that time thy people shall be delivered, every one that shall be found written in the book.

"And many of them that sleep in the dust of the earth shall awake, some to everlasting life, and some to shame and everlasting contempt.

"And they that be wise shall shine as the brightness of the firmament; and they that turn many to righteousness as the stars for ever and ever."

The first part of this revelation refers specifically to Daniel's own people, Israel, and speaks of a time of trouble even greater than any that Israel have hitherto passed through.

This is undoubtedly the same time of trouble referred to in Jeremiah chapter 30, verse 7: "Alas! for that day is great, so that none is like it: it is even the time of Jacob's trouble; but he shall be saved out of it." Jeremiah here indicates that though this time of trouble will be greater than any that Israel have previously passed through, yet they will not eventually be destroyed, but saved out of it. This agrees precisely with the statement in Daniel chapter 12, verse 1: "and at that time **thy people shall be delivered,** every one that shall be found written in the book." At this time of greatest tribulation God Himself will ultimately intervene and save that godly remnant of Israel whom in His grace He has foreknown and foreordained unto salvation.

No doubt this time of Israel's trouble is one main phase of the total period of intense trouble destined to come upon the entire world, called in the New Testament "the great tribulation".

Directly associated with this final period of tribulation is Daniel's prophecy of the resurrection, for he says in chapter 12, verse 2: "And many of them that sleep in the dust of the earth shall awake, some to everlasting life, and some to shame and everlasting contempt."

The language which Daniel here uses is closely parallel to that of Isaiah. Both alike speak of those that "dwell in the dust", both alike speak of the resurrection as an "awaking" out of the dust. However, the revelation of Daniel goes further than that of Isaiah, for Daniel indicates that there will be two distinct phases of the resurrection—one for the righteous, who will be ushered into everlasting life, and one for the wicked, who will be doomed to shame and everlasting contempt.

In chapter 12, verse 3, Daniel goes on to show that the reward of the righteous at the resurrection will be decided according to their faithfulness in serving God and in making known His truth while on earth, for he says: "And they that be wise shall shine as the brightness of the firmament; and they that turn many to righteousness as the stars forever and ever." Here there is a distinction between those who are wise to the salvation of their own souls, and those who go further than this and turn many others also to righteousness. Both alike will enter into glory, but the glory of the latter will be greater than the glory of the former.

From the passages which we have considered, we see that the theme of the resurrection runs like a thread right through the Old Testament; and that the details of this revelation become progressively clearer, until in Daniel we are told that the resurrection will be closely associated with the period of the great tribulation, and that it will occur in two distinct phases, one for the righteous and one for the wicked.

Before we close this study of Old Testament prophecies of the resurrection, there is one further point of great interest and importance which needs to be established.

In the passage already quoted from First Corinthians chapter 15, verse 3, Paul says that Christ "rose again **the third day** according to the scriptures." Not merely was the resurrection of Christ foretold in the Old Testament; it was even foretold that Christ would rise from the dead **the third day.** We may ask: Where in the Old Testament can we find this specific prophecy concerning Christ's rising again on the third day?

The answer is that this revelation is contained in Hosea chapter 6, verses 1 through 3:

"Come, and let us return unto the Lord: for he hath torn, and he will heal us; he hath smitten, and he will bind us up.

"After two days will he revive us: **in the third day** he will raise us up, and we shall live in his sight.

"Then shall we know, if we follow on to know the Lord: his going forth is prepared as the morning; and he shall come unto us as the rain, as the latter and former rain unto the earth."

This prophecy commences with a promise of forgiveness and healing to those who will return to the Lord in repentance and faith.

Then, in the second verse, comes the clear prophecy of the resurrection on the third day: "**in the third day** he will raise us up, and we shall live in his sight." We notice that this promise is given in the plural, not the singular: "he will raise **us** up"—"**we** shall live in his sight." That is to say, the promise refers not merely to the resurrection of Christ Himself, but it also includes all those who obey the exhortation of the previous verse to return to God in repentance and faith.

In order to understand fully the truth contained in this prophecy, we must turn to the complete revelation of the gospel as given by God to the church through the apostle Paul in the New Testament.

In Romans chapter 6, verse 6, Paul says: "Our old man is crucified with him—that is, with Christ."

Again, in Galatians chapter 2, verse 20, Paul says: "I am crucified with Christ."

These, and other similar passages, reveal that in making atonement for man's sin, Christ deliberately made Himself one with the sinner. He took the sinner's guilt; He made Himself one with the sinner's corrupt and fallen nature; He died the sinner's death; He paid the sinner's penalty.

Thereafter, it remains for us, as sinners, to accept by faith our identification with Christ. When we do this, we find that we are identified with Him not merely in His death and burial, but also in His resurrection from the dead and in the new immortal, resurrection life which He now enjoys.

This aspect of our identification with Christ is stated by Paul in Ephesians, chapter 2, verses 4 through 6, where he says: "God . . . hath quickened us together with Christ (that is, made us alive together with Christ) . . . and hath raised up together (that is, from the dead), and made us sit together in heavenly places in Christ Jesus."

As soon as we are willing, by faith, to accept our identification with Christ in His death for our sins, we find that we are also identified with Christ in His resurrection and in His new victorious life upon God's throne. Entering in through His death, we become partakers also of His resurrection.

The same truth is contained also in the words of Jesus Himself to His disciples in John chapter 14, verse 19: "Because I live, ye shall live also."

For this reason, the prophetic revelation states in Hosea chapter 6, verse 2: "in the third day he will raise us up, and we shall live in his sight." This prophecy reveals not merely that Christ was to be raised on the third day, but also that, according to God's eternal purpose in the gospel, all those who believed in Christ were to be identified with Him in His resurrection. In this respect, Hosea's prophecy is characteristic of Old Testament prophecy as a whole, in that it not merely predicts an event which is to take place, but at the same time it also reveals the true spiritual significance of that event, and its connection with God's whole purpose in the gospel.

However, Hosea also warns that this secret of God's purpose in the resurrection of Christ will be revealed only to those who are willing to seek the truth with faith and diligence, for he says in the next verse: "Then shall we know, if we follow on to know the Lord." This revelation is only for those who "follow on to know the Lord."

For those who do thus follow on, Hosea continues, "his going forth is prepared as the morning." That is, the resurrection of Christ from the dead is as sure and certain in God's purpose as the rising of the sun after the darkness of night. This is closely parallel to the prophecy of Christ's resurrection in Malachi chapter 4, verse 2: "But unto you that fear my name shall the Sun of righteousness arise with healing in his wings." Again we notice a limitation of those to whom this revelation of the risen Christ will be granted: it is not for all men, but "unto you that fear my name".

Finally, Hosea indicates that the resurrection of Christ will be closely followed by the outpouring of the Holy Spirit, for he goes on: "and he shall come unto us as the rain, as the latter and former rain unto the earth." The "rain" is here a figure of the Holy Spirit's outpouring, divided into two main visitations—the former rain, and the latter rain.

In accurate fulfilment of this prophecy, the New Testament records that on the day of Pentecost, fifty days after Christ's resurrection, the former rain of the Holy Spirit began to be poured out upon His waiting disciples—those who had "followed on to know the Lord."

We may therefore sum up these Old Testament prophecies which we have examined, as follows. The Old Testament clearly foretells: first, that Christ Himself will be raised from the dead; second, that those who believe in Christ will share His resurrection; third, that there will also be a resurrection of the wicked for purposes of judgment and punishment.

*   *   *

In our next study we shall examine various passages in the New Testament, which not only confirm these Old Testament prophecies, but also make the whole picture of the resurrection clearer and more detailed.

V
"Christb The Firstfruits"

Three Successive Phases Of Resurrection—Christ's Resurrection Fulfils The Typology Of The Firstfruits

Welcome to the Study Hour.

Our textbook - the Bible.

The study which we shall now bring you is Number 44 in our present series, entitled "Foundations".

We are at present examining that doctrine of the Christian faith which is called, in Hebrews chapter 6, verse 2, "resurrection of the dead".

In our last study we examined some of the main passages of the Old Testament which prophetically foreshow the resurrection, and we saw that the Old Testament clearly foretells the following three main facts concerning the resurrection: first, that Christ Himself will be raised from the dead; second, that those who believe in Christ will share His resurrection; third, that there will also be a resurrection of the wicked for purposes of judgment and punishment.

If we now turn on to the New Testament, we shall find that the revelation there given concerning the resurrection agrees exactly in these three main points with that of the Old Testament; but that a good deal of further information is also given, to make the whole picture of the resurrection clearer and more detailed.

The first New Testament passage which we shall consider is found in John chapter 5. Jesus Himself is here speaking, and in John chapter 5, verse 25, He says:

"Verily, verily, I say unto you, The hour is coming, and now is, when **the dead** shall hear the voice of the Son of God: and they that hear shall live."

A little further on, in verses 28 and 29, Jesus says again:

"Marvel not at this: for the hour is coming, in the which **all that are in the graves** shall hear his voice,

"And shall come forth; they that have done good, unto the resurrection of life; and they that have done evil, unto the resurrection of damnation."

Jesus here uses two different phrases. In verse 25, He says "the dead"; in verse 28, He says "all that are in the graves". The context seems to indicate that these two phrases are not identical, but are contrasted with each other.

If this is so, then the first phrase, "the dead", must be taken to describe not those who are actually physically dead, but rather those who are spiritually dead in sin. This is in line with the language used by Paul in the Epistle to the Ephesians.

For example, in Ephesians chapter 2, verse 1, Paul says: "And you hath God quickened—that is, made alive—who were dead in trespasses and sin." Here the whole context makes it plain that Paul is not speaking about people who were literally, physically dead, but about people who, as a result of sin, were spiritually dead and alienated from God.

Again in Ephesians chapter 5, verse 14, Paul quotes from Isaiah a passage which he applies as an exhortation to the sinner: "Awake thou that sleepest, and arise from the dead, and Christ shall give thee light." Here, too, the one whom Paul exhorts to "awake, and arise from the dead," is not physically dead, but spiritually dead in sin.

It would seem therefore that we should apply this interpretation to the words of Jesus in John chapter 5, verse 25: "Verily, verily, I say unto you, The hour is coming, and now is, when **the dead** shall hear the voice of the Son of God: and they that hear shall live."

Thus, Jesus is here speaking about the response of those who are dead in sin to the voice of Christ, brought to them through the preaching of the gospel: "They that hear shall live." That is, those who receive the gospel message with faith shall thereby receive forgiveness and eternal life.

This is confirmed by the fact that Jesus says concerning this: "The hour is coming, **and now is**." That is to say, the preaching of the gospel to men dead in sins had already commenced at the time that Jesus spoke these words.

We notice the contrast between this and the words of Jesus in John chapter 5, verses 28 and 29: "the hour is coming, in which **all that are in the graves** shall hear his voice, and shall come forth; they that have done good, unto the resurrection of life; and they that have done evil, unto the resurrection of damnation."

This passage differs from the previous one in three main respects.

First, Jesus says, "the hour is coming", but He does not add, "and now is". That is to say, the events of which Jesus here speaks are still entirely in the future; they have not yet begun to be fulfilled.

Second, Jesus uses the phrase, "all that are in the graves". This clearly refers to those who have actually died and been buried. Furthermore, He says that **all** these, without exception, will hear; whereas in the previous passage, concerning "the dead", He indicated that only some would hear, not all.

Third, in this second passage, Jesus actually uses the word "resurrection". He says that all those in the graves will "come forth **unto resurrection**".

We conclude therefore that in the first passage Jesus is speaking about the response of those who are spiritually dead in sin; while in the second passage He is speaking about the literal resurrection of those who have actually died and been buried.

The teaching of Jesus in this second passage concerning the resurrection agrees exactly with the Old Testament revelation given in Daniel chapter 12, verses 1 through 3. In each case, the resurrection is spoken of in two distinct phases, that of the righteous, and that of the wicked; and in each case, the resurrection of the righteous precedes that of the wicked. In addition, we learn from the words of Jesus one further point not revealed in Daniel: the voice that will call all the dead forth to resurrection will be that of Christ Himself, the Son of God.

If we now turn on to First Corinthians chapter 15, we find there a yet fuller and more detailed account of the resurrection. In First Corinthians chapter 15, verses 22 through 24, Paul says:

"For as in Adam all die, even so in Christ shall all be made alive.

"But every man in his own order: Christ the firstfruits; afterward they that are Christ's at his coming.

"Then cometh the end, when he (Christ) shall have delivered up the kingdom to God, even the Father; when he shall have put down all rule and all authority and power."

Notice the phrase: "every man in his own order". The word translated "order" is used to describe a "rank" of soldiers. Thus, Paul here pictures the resurrection as occurring in three successive stages, like three ranks of soldiers marching past, one behind the other.

The first stage consists of Christ Himself—"Christ the firstfruits".

The second stage consist of all true Christians at the time of Christ's return—"they that are Christ's at his coming". This corresponds to the resurrection of the righteous, as foretold in Daniel and by Christ Himself.

The third stage is called "the end"—that is, the end of Christ's earthly reign of one thousand years, at the close of which He will deliver up the kingdom to God the Father. Of those resurrected at this stage, the majority—but not all—will belong to the resurrection of the wicked, as foretold in Daniel and by Christ. Concerning this third stage, Paul says nothing more here in First Corinthians. However, we shall see in due course that further details concerning this are given in Revelation chapter 20.

In the meanwhile, let us examine more closely what Paul here says about the first two stages.

The first stage, Paul says, is "Christ the firstfruits".

By this phrase, Paul compares the resurrection of Christ to the ceremony of presenting the firstfruits of the harvest to the Lord, as ordained for the children of Israel under the law of Moses. This ceremony is described in Leviticus chapter 23, verses 10 and 11:

"Speak unto the children of Israel, and say unto them, When ye be come into the land which I give unto you, and shall reap the harvest thereof, then ye shall bring a sheaf of the firstfruits of your harvest unto the priest:

"And he shall wave the sheaf before the Lord, to be accepted for you: on the morrow after the sabbath the priest shall wave it."

This sheaf of the firstfruits waved before the Lord is a picture of Christ coming forth from the dead as the sinner's representative and as the beginning of a new creation.

Notice how accurate the picture is. The sheaf of the firstfruits was the first complete fruit to rise up out of the seed that had been buried earlier in the earth. Moses told the children of Israel that the priest was to wave this sheaf before the Lord, "**to be accepted for you.**" In Romans chapter 4, verse 25, Paul tells us that Christ "was delivered for our offences, and was **raised again for our justification.**" The resurrection of Christ not merely vindicated His own righteousness; it also made it possible for the believer to be reckoned equally righteous with Christ before God.

Furthermore, this sheaf of the firstfruits was to be waved before the Lord "on the morrow after the sabbath". Since the sabbath was the seventh, or last day of the week, "the morrow after the sabbath" was the first day of the week— the day on which Christ did in fact rise from the dead.

Finally, the waving of the firstfruits was an act of worship and of triumph, for the appearing of the firstfruits at the appointed season gave assurance that the rest of the harvest would be gathered safely in. In like manner, the resurrection of Christ gives assurance that all the remaining dead will also in their due season be resurrected.

However, there is yet one further prophetic revelation concerning Christ's resurrection contained in this Old Testament ordinance of the firstfruits.

In John chapter 12, verse 24, Jesus speaks prophetically of His own impending death and burial, and He compares this to a corn of wheat being buried in the earth. He says: "Verily, verily, I say unto you, Except a corn of wheat fall into the ground and die, it abideth alone: but if it die, it bringeth forth much fruit."

By this Jesus taught that the fruit of His ministry of reconciliation between God and man could come only as a result of His own atoning death and resurrection. If He were to stop short of the death of the cross, no fruit could come forth out of His ministry. It was only through His death, burial and resurrection that there could come forth the fruit of a great harvest of sinners justified and reconciled to God. This truth He presented to His disciples under the picture of a corn of wheat being buried in the earth, germinating, and springing up again as a fruitful stalk out of the earth.

However, it is a fact of nature that, although a single corn of wheat is buried in the earth, the stalk which springs up out of that single corn never bears merely one single corn, but a whole head, or cluster, of corns upon the one stalk. In short, a corn never brings forth a single corn, but a whole cluster containing many corns. As Jesus Himself indicated in the parable of the sower, the ratio of increase out of the single corn may be thirtyfold, or sixtyfold, or a hundredfold.

This truth of natural law applies also in the spiritual counterpart of Christ's resurrection. Jesus was buried alone, but He did not rise alone. This fact, which has received surprisingly little attention from the majority of Bible commentators, is clearly stated in Matthew chapter 27, verses 50 through 53. These verses record the death of Jesus upon the cross, and various events connected therewith, which followed upon His death and resurrection. The record is as follows:

"Jesus, when he had cried again with a loud voice, yielded up the ghost.

"And, behold, the veil of the temple was rent in twain from the top to the bottom; and the earth did quake, and the rocks rent;

"And the graves were opened; and many bodies of the saints which slept arose,

"And came out of the graves after his resurrection, and went into the holy city, and appeared unto many."

Though these events are here presented in close succession one after the other, it is clear that the total period of time which they covered extended over three days. The death of Jesus on the cross took place on the eve of the sabbath; but his resurrection took place early in the morning of the first day of the new week. In connection with this, Matthew states, "the graves were opened; and many bodies of the saints which slept arose, and came out of the graves **after his resurrection** . . . " At what precise moment the graves were opened, we do not clearly know; but we do know that it was only after the resurrection of Christ Himself that these resurrected saints arose and came out of their graves.

In this way, the Old Testament type of the firstfruits was perfectly fulfilled by the resurrection of Christ. Christ was buried alone—a single corn of wheat that fell into the ground. But when He arose again from the dead, He was no longer alone—no longer one single corn. Instead, there was a handful—a sheaf of the firstfruits—brought forth together with Him out of the dead, and waved in triumph before God as a token of the defeat of Satan and hell and all the forces of darkness, and as an assurance that all others who had been buried would also in their due season be resurrected.

Concerning these Old Testament saints resurrected at this time together with Jesus, two interesting questions naturally suggest themselves.

The first question is this: Did these resurrected saints comprise **all** the righteous believers of the Old Testament? Were **all** the Old Testament saints resurrected at this time together with Jesus?

To this question, the answer would appear to be "No." The first reason for this is found in the words of Matthew himself. Matthew says: **"Many** bodies of the saints which slept arose." This phrase, "many . . . of the saints," in normal usage would indicate that it was **not all** the saints that arose.

This conclusion is further supported by the words of Peter on the day of Pentecost, as recorded in Acts chapter 2, verse 29, where he says: "Men and brethren, let me freely speak unto you of the patriarch David, that he is both dead and buried, and his sepulchre is with us unto this day." Peter is here speaking fifty days after the resurrection of Christ. Yet his words plainly indicate that the dead body of David was still in his tomb at that time. This shows that David, one of the greatest of the Old Testament saints, had not yet been resurrected at the time when Peter spoke on the day of Pentecost; and therefore that this resurrection of Old Testament saints on the first Easter Sunday morning was a resurrection of some, but not of all.

The second interesting question concerning these resurrected Old Testament saints is this: What became of them after their resurrection?

From the account given, it would appear that these Old Testament saints were, in the true sense, "resurrected"— that is, they were raised up once and for all out of the dominion of death and the grave, never to return again under that dominion. In this respect, there is a complete difference between these saints and the people whom Jesus raised from the dead during His earthly ministry. Those whom Christ raised from the dead were merely called back, out of death, to the same kind of natural, earthly life, which they had previously had. They still remained liable to all the weaknesses of mortal flesh, and in due course they died again, and were buried. These people had merely been restored to natural, earthly life; they had not been resurrected from the dead. On the other hand, the saints who rose with Jesus shared His resurrection with Him. They entered into a totally new kind of life; they received new, spiritual bodies, just like that which Jesus Himself received.

This is indicated by the words of Matthew chapter 27, verse 53, where it is stated concerning these resurrected saints, that "they came out of the graves after his resurrection, and went into the holy city (that is, Jerusalem), and **appeared** unto many." These words indicate that these saints had bodies of the same kind that Jesus Himself had after His resurrection. They could appear, or disappear, at will. They were no longer subject to the physical limitations of a normal, earthly body. If this is so, then there can be no thought that they ever returned again into their graves, and submitted themselves afresh to the process of decomposition. In putting on these resurrection bodies, they had passed once and for all out of the shadow and the dominion of death and the grave, never to return thereunder again.

What became of these saints after this? It does not appear that there is any definite or final answer to this question given in the New Testament. However, it seems natural to suppose that these saints, having shared with Jesus in His resurrection, shared with Him also in His ascension into heaven. Let us therefore glance for a moment at the description of the ascension of Jesus into heaven, as given in the New Testament. This is found in Acts chapter 1, verse 9: "And when he had spoken these things, while they beheld, he was taken up; and a cloud received him out of their sight."

We notice that Jesus passed out of his disciples' sight into a cloud, and that within this cloud He then continued His ascent to heaven. Immediately after this, in Acts chapter 1, verse 11, we read that two angels appeared to the disciples and gave them the following assurance concerning the return of Christ: "This same Jesus, which is taken up from you into heaven, shall so come in like manner as ye have seen him go into heaven." This teaches that there is to be a close parallel between the ascent of Christ into heaven and His return again from heaven to earth: "He shall so come in like manner" as He was seen to go.

Concerning the return of Christ from heaven, two facts are clearly stated. In Mark chapter 13, verse 26—and in other passages also—it is stated that Christ will come again "in the clouds"—more literally, "in clouds". Again, in Zechariah chapter 14, verse 5, and in Jude verse 14, it is stated that Christ will come "with his saints".

Combining these two statements, we find that Christ will come "in clouds", "with His saints". We know also that the ascension of Christ into heaven and His return from heaven are closely parallel. We know, further, that Christ ascended into heaven "in a cloud". We are therefore merely completing the parallel, if we suggest that Christ ascended into heaven together with those of His saints who had at that time been resurrected.

There is one further point of interest to notice in this connection. In Hebrews chapter 12, verse 1, the writer says: "Wherefore seeing we also are compassed about with so great a **cloud** of witnesses, let us lay aside every weight, and the sin which doth so easily beset us, and let us run with patience the race that is set before us . . . "

What is this "cloud of witnesses" to which the writer of Hebrews here refers? The context makes it plain that the writer here refers to the various Old Testament saints, whose exploits of faith had been recorded in the previous chapter—that is, Hebrews chapter 11. Thus these Old Testament saints are here pictured as a cloud of witnesses surrounding each Christian believer who undertakes to run the race of faith in this dispensation. In this way, we find the figure of a cloud once again linked to the saints of the Old Testament.

From all these considerations, it seems both logical and scriptural to suggest that, on the day of His ascension, Jesus was taken up into heaven within a cloud that contained within it those of the Old Testament saints who had at that time been resurrected. In this way, the resurrection and ascension of Christ would most exactly and completely fulfil all that is indicated in the typology of the Old Testament ordinance of the firstfruits. It would also be exactly parallel to the method of His promised return from heaven to earth.

However, this conclusion should be considered as being no more than a logical inference from various indications of scripture. It should not be put forward dogmatically as an established doctrine.

*   *   *

In our next study we shall go on to examine the second main phase of the resurrection, referred to by Paul as "they that are Christ's at his coming".

VI
"They That Are Christ's At His Coming"

Five Main Purposes Of Christ's Second Coming—Resurrection And Rapture Of True Believers—The Two Witnesses And The Tribulation Martyrs

Welcome to the Study Hour.

Our textbook - the Bible.

The study which we shall now bring you is Number 45 in our present series, entitled "Foundations".

We are at present examining that doctrine of the Christian faith which is called, in Hebrews chapter 6, verse 2, "resurrection of the dead".

We have seen that the Bible reveals that the resurrection takes place in three main distinct and successive phases. These three phases are stated by Paul, in First Corinthians chapter 15, verses 23 and 24, as follows: "Christ the firstfruits (that is, the first phase); afterward they that are Christ's at his coming (that is, the second phase). Then cometh the end (that is, the third and final phase) . . . "

In our last study we considered the first phase of the resurrection, called by Paul "Christ the firstfruits"; and we saw how exactly and completely the account of Christ's resurrection given in the New Testament fulfilled the prophetic typology of the ordinance of the firstfruits, as ordained for Israel in the Old Testament.

In our present study we shall now go on to consider the the second main phase of the resurrection—that which Paul refers to as "they that are Christ's at his coming".

It is important to notice carefully the exact phrases which Paul here uses concerning this second phase of the resurrection. First of all, the Greek word here translated "coming" is "parousia". This is the word mainly used throughout the New Testament to denote that aspect of Christ's second coming which primarily concerns the church— that is, Christ's coming as the Bridegroom to take His bride, the church, to Himself.

Secondly, we must notice how carefully Paul specifies just exactly those that will take part in this second phase of the resurrection. He says "they that are Christ's". This phrase indicates possession. It is equivalent to saying "those who belong to Christ". This certainly does not include all those who make a profession of faith in Christ. It covers only those who have so fully and unreservedly yielded themselves to Christ that they are entirely His. They are no longer their own; they belong to Christ.

In Ephesians chapter 1, verse 14, Paul speaks about this aspect of Christ's coming for His church as "the redemption of the **purchased possession**". Only those Christians can take part in this phase of resurrection who are already a part of Christ's "purchased possession"—those who have allowed Christ to take full possession of all that they are and all that they have. Christ comes, it is true, "like a thief", but He certainly does not come to steal. He comes to take to Himself only those who are already "His own". There is no place in this phase of resurrection for those who merely profess faith in Christ, but have never yielded themselves wholly to Him in full surrender and obedience.

With this clear warning in mind, let us consider what the New Testament reveals will take place at this second main phase of the resurrection. Since Paul states that this will take place "at Christ's coming", it is clear that this second phase of the resurrection is directly associated with the return of Christ. Now the return of Christ is one of the main themes of all Biblical prophecy. Someone has estimated that, for every one promise in the Bible concerning the first coming of Christ, there are at least five promises concerning His second coming. This shows how great a part the theme of the second coming of Christ plays in the total revelation of scripture. For this reason, it is outside the scope of our present studies to discuss in detail the whole question of Christ's second coming. It is, however, helpful to point out that, in the eternal purposes of God, the second coming of Christ is intended to accomplish a number of different purposes. These purposes are in some sense distinct from each other, yet all interrelated in God's overall plan. Each of these purposes constitutes one main aspect of Christ's second coming, one main phase of the total event as foreshown in scripture.

Briefly, we may mention the following **five** main purposes for which Christ will come again.

First, Christ will come for the church. He will come again, as the Bridegroom, to receive unto Himself all true believers, as His bride. All true believers will be united with Christ, either by resurrection, or by an instantaneous change in their bodies while still alive. One passage where this is clearly stated is John chapter 14, verse 3, where Jesus says to His disciples: "And if I go and prepare a place for you, I will come again, and receive you unto myself; that where I am, there ye may be also."

Second, Christ will come for the national salvation of Israel. The national remnant of Israel that will have survived the fires of the great tribulation, will acknowledge Jesus Christ as their Messiah, and will thus be reconciled to God and restored to His favour and blessing. This is clearly foreshown in the promise of God, through Isaiah, quoted by Paul in Romans chapter 11, verses 26 and 27:

"And so all Israel shall be saved: as it is written, there shall come out of Zion the Deliverer, and shall turn away ungodliness from Jacob:

"For this is my covenant unto them, when I shall take away their sins."

Third, Christ will come for the overthrow of anti-Christ, and of Satan himself. One passage foretelling this is found in Second Thessalonians chapter 2, verse 8: "And then shall that Wicked (the anti-Christ) be revealed, whom the Lord shall consume with the spirit of his mouth, and shall destroy with the brightness of his coming."

Fourth, Christ will come for the judgment of the Gentile nations. This is foretold in Matthew chapter 25, verses 31 and 32:

"When the Son of man shall come in his glory, and all the holy angels with him, then shall he sit upon the throne of his glory:

"And before him shall be gathered all nations: and he shall separate them one from another, as a shepherd divideth his sheep from the goats: . . . "

Fifth, Christ will come for the establishment of His millennial kingdom upon the earth. This is prophesied in Isaiah chapter 24, verse 23: "Then the moon shall be confounded, and the sun ashamed, when the Lord of hosts shall reign in mount Zion, and in Jerusalem, and before his ancients gloriously." The period of time for which Christ shall thus reign is given in Revelation chapter 20, verse 4, where it says concerning the martyrs of the tribulation period: "and they lived and reigned with Christ a thousand years."

Thus, we may briefly summarise the five main purposes for which Christ will come, as follows:

First, Christ will come for the church, to receive all true believers to Himself.

Second, Christ will come for the national salvation of Israel.

Third, Christ will come for the overthrow of anti-Christ and of Satan himself.

Fourth, Christ will come for the judgment of the Gentile nations.

Fifth, Christ will come to establish His millennial kingdom upon earth.

While there is a fair measure of agreement amongst Bible believers concerning these main purposes of Christ's second coming, there has been much discussion and controversy concerning the details of these various phases of Christ's return, and the precise relationship of each phase to all the rest. Some of the main questions that have been asked are as follows: Will all these phases of Christ's return together constitute one single event? Or will there be definite intervals of time between some of them? If so, in what order will they take place? Is it possible that some phases will partly overlap others?

So far as possible, in our present study, we shall seek to avoid entering unnecessarily into these controversial questions, and to confine ourselves to that particular aspect of Christ's return which is directly associated with the resurrection of the righteous.

The main passage of the new Testament which describes that phase of the resurrection which will take place at Christ's coming is found in First Thessalonians chapter 4, verses 13 through 18:

"But I would not have you to be ignorant, brethren, concerning them which are asleep, that ye sorrow not, even as others which have no hope.

"For if we believe that Jesus died and rose again, even so them also which sleep in Jesus will God bring with him.

"For this we say unto you by the word of the Lord, that

we which are alive and remain unto the coming of the Lord shall not prevent them which are asleep.

"For the Lord himself shall descend from heaven with a shout, with the voice of the archangel, and with the trump of God: and the dead in Christ shall rise first:

"Then we which are alive and remain shall be caught up together with them in the clouds, to meet the Lord in the air: and so shall we ever be with the Lord.

"Wherefore comfort one another with these words."

The primary purpose of Paul's teaching here is to comfort Christian believers concerning other Christians—relatives or other loved ones—who have died. These Christians who have died are described as "them which are asleep"; or, more precisely, "them which sleep in Jesus". This means those that have died in the faith of the gospel. Paul's message of comfort is based on the assurance that these, and all other true believers, will be resurrected.

The actual picture which Paul gives of this phase of the resurrection is as follows.

First, there will be three dramatic sounds to herald this phase of resurrection. The first sound will be the shout of the Lord Jesus Christ Himself. This is in agreement with the words of Jesus Himself in John chapter 5, verses 28 and 29: "all that are in the graves shall hear his voice, and shall come forth; they that have done good unto the resurrection of life; and they that have done evil, unto the resurrection of damnation." It is the voice of Christ Himself alone that has power to call the dead out of their graves. However, at this particular moment He will call forth only the righteous dead—only those that have died in the faith. The calling forth of the unrighteous dead will be reserved for a later phase of resurrection.

The other two sounds that will be heard at this point will be "the voice of the archangel, and the trumpet of God." The archangel here referred to is probably Gabriel, since it appears to be his special ministry to proclaim upon earth impending interventions of God in the affairs of men. All through the Bible, one main use of the trumpet is to gather the Lord's people together in any special time of crisis. Thus the sound of the trumpet at this point will be the signal for all the Lord's people to gather together with Him, as He Himself descends from heaven to meet them.

Upon earth two great events will occur in swift succession. First, all true believers who have died in the faith will be resurrected. Second, all true believers alive on earth at that moment will undergo an instantaneous, supernatural change in their bodies.

Then both these companies of believers—those that were resurrected, and those whose bodies were changed without dying—will together be swiftly raised by God's supernatural power from the earth up into the air. There they will be received into clouds, and within these clouds they will be reunited with their Lord and with each other. Thereafter the Lord and His redeemed believers shall for ever be united in the unbroken harmony and fellowship of heaven.

In studying this account of the resurrection and rapture of true believers, it is interesting to notice the meaning of two of the Greek words used in the original text. Paul says: "we shall be **caught up**". The Greek word translated "to catch up" is "harpazo". The root meaning of this verb denotes a sudden, swift, violent grab. It is used four times in the New Testament to describe people being caught up to heaven. In addition, it is used in Acts chapter 8, verse 39, where we read that "the Spirit of the Lord caught away Philip" from the Ethiopian ennuch. It is used by Jesus Himself in John chapter 10, verse 12, to describe the wolf "catching" the sheep. It is used by Him also in Matthew chapter 13, verse 19, to describe the birds "catching away" the seed sown by the wayside. It is used in Jude, verse 23, to describe people being "pulled" out of the fire.

Thus the use of this verb is deliberately intended to give an impression of one single, swift, sudden, violent act. Indeed it suggests particularly the act of a thief. In this respect it is in line with other scriptures which compare this aspect of Christ's coming to that of a thief. For example, in Revelation chapter 16, verse 15, Jesus says: "Behold, I come as a thief." And again, in Matthew chapter 24, verses 42 and 43, He says:

"Watch therefore: for ye know not what hour your Lord doth come.

"But know this, that if the goodman of the house had known in what watch **the thief** would come, he would have watched, and would not have suffered his house to be broken up."

Notice the suggestion of violence in the statement that the house is to be "**broken up**".

Thus we may say that the coming of Christ for His church at this point will be like that of a thief in the following respects. It will be sudden, unexpected, without warning; it will culminate in one single, ruthless act of snatching away. Furthermore, that which is to be snatched away will be earth's most valuable treasure—the true Christians.

However, as we have already said, Christ's coming will differ from that of a thief in one extremely important respect. He will take away only that which is already His own by right of redemption.

If we now turn back again to First Thessalonians chapter 4, verse 17, we may consider one other interesting word used in the Greek. Paul says that we shall meet the Lord "**in the air**". The Greek word here used is "aer". This is on of two Greek words normally translated "air". The other word is "aither". The difference between these two words is that "aer" denotes the lower air, in immediate contact with the earth's surface; "aither" denotes the higher, rarer air, some considerable distance above the earth's surface. Since Paul uses the word "aer" in relation to the Lord's return, he indicates thereby that the Lord's gathering together with His raptured saints will take place in the lower air, quite close to the earth's surface.

Paul refers again to this same moment of resurrection and rapture in First Corinthians, chapter 15, verses 51 and 52, where he says:

"Behold, I shew you a mystery; We shall not all sleep, but we shall all be changed,

"In a moment, in the twinkling of an eye, at the last trump: for the trumpet shall sound, and the dead shall be raised incorruptible, and we shall be changed."

Paul here unfolds "a mystery"—that is a previously unrevealed secret of God's plan for the church. The secret thus revealed is this: all true believers will be raptured together at the Lord's coming, but not all those to be raptured will have died and been resurrected. Those who are alive at the Lord's coming will not die at all, but will simply undergo an instantaneous and miraculous change in their bodies. By this change their bodies will be rendered exactly like those of the other believers who have been resurrected from the dead.

In the next verse Paul briefly summarises the nature of the change that will take place: "For this corruptible must put on incorruption, and this mortal must put on immortality." Instead of being mortal and corruptible, the new body of each believer will be immortal and incorruptible.

Does this account here given by Paul constitute a complete picture of the resurrection of all Christian believers before the establishment of Christ's kingdom in the millennium?

To this question the answer would appear to be "No." For it would seem that at least two further phases of the resurrection of the righteous are recorded in the Book of Revelation.

In Revelation chapter 11, we read the account of God's two witnesses during the tribulation period, and of their eventual martyrdom by "the beast that ascendeth out of the bottomless pit"—that is, the anti-Christ. In verses 9, 11 and 12 of this chapter the account continues as follows:

"And they of the people and kindreds and tongues and nations shall see their dead bodies three days and an half, and shall not suffer their dead bodies to be put in graves. . .

"And after three days and an half the spirit of life from God entered into them, and they stood upon their feet . . .

"And they heard a great voice from heaven saying unto them, Come up hither. And they ascended up to heaven in a cloud; and their enemies beheld them."

The account makes it plain that this in the fullest sense is a "resurrection". Although their bodies had not been buried, these two martyrs had been dead for three and a half days. Then, in the open sight of their enemies, their bodies were resurrected, and they ascended into heaven. It is very interesting to notice that their ascension into heaven is similar to each of the other cases that we have already considered, in that it takes place "**in a cloud**".

If we now turn on to Revelation chapter 20, verses 4 through 6, we find the account of a further resurrection of the righteous:

"And I saw thrones, and they sat on them, and judgment was given unto them: and I saw the souls of them that were beheaded for the witness of Jesus, and for the word of God, and which had not worshipped the beast, neither his image, neither had received his mark upon their foreheads, or in their hands; and they lived and reigned with Christ a thousand years.

"But the rest of the dead lived not again until the thousand years were finished. This is the first resurrection.

"Blessed and holy is he that hath part in the first resurrection . . . "

It is clear that the people whose resurrection is here described are those who died by beheading as martyrs of Jesus during the period of the rule of anti-Christ. These tribulation saints are here shown as being resurrected at the close of the great tribulation, just prior to the establishment of Christ's millennial kingdom. They thus share with Christ Himself, and with all other resurrected saints, in the privilege of ruling and judging the nations on earth during the period of the millennium.

John the Revelator closes the account of the resurrection of these martyrs with the words: "This is the first resurrection. Blessed and holy is he that hath part in the first resurrection . . . "

By these words John apparently indicates that "the first resurrection" is now complete. All those who take part in this resurrection are called "blessed and holy". That is to say, those who take part in this resurrection are all righteous believers. Up to this point, none of the unrighteous have as yet been resurrected. The second resurrection, in which the unrighteous have their part, is described by John in the latter part of Revelation chapter 20.

If we now combine together the revelations given by Paul and by John, we may make the following summary of the resurrection of the righteous.

The total resurrection of the righteous, from the moment of Christ's own resurrection down to the resurrection of the tribulation martyrs just prior to the millennium, is called by John "the first resurrection". All those who take part in this resurrection are "blessed and holy"; that is, they are all righteous believers.

However, within this total resurrection of the righteous we may discern at least four successive phases. These four phases are as follows:

First, "Christ the firstfruits"—that is, Christ Himself and those of the Old Testament saints who were resurrected at the time of Christ's resurrection.

Second, "they that are Christ's at his coming"—the true believers who are ready to meet Christ at His return, together with those who had died in the faith—all these together being caught up in clouds to meet Christ in the air.

Third, the two witnesses of the tribulation period, who are left dead but unburied for three and a half days, and are then resurrected and ascend to heaven in a cloud.

Fourth, the remainder of the tribulation martyrs, who are resurrected at the close of the tribulation period, in time to share with Christ Himself and the other saints in the privilege of ruling and judging the nations on earth during the millennium.

Such, in brief outline, is the picture that the New Testament gives of the resurrection of the righteous.

*　　*　　*

In our next study, we shall go on to consider the final, closing phase of the resurrection.

VII
"Then Cometh The End"

*Events At The Close Of The Millennium—The Personality
Of Death And Hell—The Two "Whosoevers"*

Welcome to the Study Hour.

Our textbook - the Bible.

The study which we shall now bring you is Number 46
in our present series, entitled "Foundations".

We are at present examining that doctrine of the Christian faith which is called, in Hebrews chapter 6, verse 2,
"resurrection of the dead".

In our two previous studies we have considered that part
of the total plan of resurrection which is called "the first
resurrection". We have seen that this "first resurrection"
extends from the moment of Christ's own resurrection down
to the resurrection of the tribulation martyrs just prior to
the millennium. All those who take part in this resurrection
are called "blessed and holy"—that is, they are all righteous
believers.

However, within this total resurrection of the righteous
we discerned the following four main successive phases:

First, "Christ the firstfruits"—that is, Christ Himself and
those of the Old Testament saints who were resurrected at
the time of Christ's resurrection.

Second, "they that are Christ's at his coming"—the true
believers who are ready to meet Christ at His return, together with those who had died in the faith—all these together being caught up in clouds to meet Christ in the air.

Third, the two witnesses of the tribulation period, who
are left dead but unburied for three and a half days, and
are then resurrected and ascend to heaven in a cloud.

Fourth, the remainder of the tribulation martyrs, who
are resurrected at the close of the tribulation period, in time
to share with Christ Himself and the other saints in the
privilege of ruling and judging the nations on earth during
the millennium.

In our present study we shall now go on to consider
the final, closing phase of the resurrection. The manner in

which this last phase of the resurrection will take place is indicated by Paul in First Corinthians chapter 15, verses 23 through 26:

"But every man in his own order: Christ the firstfruits; afterward they that are Christ's at his coming.

"Then cometh the end, when he (Christ) shall have delivered up the kingdom to God, even the Father; when he shall have put down all rule and all authority and power.

"For he must reign, till he hath put all enemies under his feet.

"The last enemy that shall be destroyed is death."

Here, in verse 23, Paul indicates the two main stages of "the first resurrection"—that is, "Christ the firstfruits", and then "they that are Christ's at his coming".

Then, in verse 24, Paul moves on to the final stage of the resurrection. This he refers to in the phrase, "then cometh the end." He goes on to indicate the other main events that will be associated with this final stage of the resurrection. By this time Christ will have completed His earthly reign of one thousand years. By the completion of this period of one thousand years, God the Father will have brought all Christ's enemies into subjection to Christ. The last of these enemies to be brought into final subjection will be death. Thereafter, Christ, the Son, will in turn offer up His kingdom to God the Father; and will, in accordance with His position as the Son, voluntarily place Himself in subjection to His Father's rule and authority.

This closing phase of Christ's earthly rule is described by Paul two verses further on, in First Corinthians chapter 15, verse 28: "And when all things shall be subdued unto him (that is, Christ), then shall the Son also himself be subject unto him that put all things under him, that God may be all in all."

As we study this prophetic picture of "the end", we notice the perfect harmony that exists, within the Godhead, between the Father and the Son. First, God the Father will, during the millennium, establish Christ, the Son, as His appointed Representative and Ruler over all things; and by the close of this period the Father will have brough all Christ's enemies into subjection unto Him—the last enemy being death. Thereafter, Christ, the Son, will in turn offer up, in subjection to the authority of the Father, both Himself and all that the Father has made subject to Him. In this way, Paul says, God the Father, through Christ, will be "all in all".

This offering up of the completed kingdom by Christ to the Father represents the climax and culmination of God's plan for all the ages. Paul refers to this glorious culmination of God's purpose also in Ephesians chapter 1, verses 9 and 10, where he tells us that God has "made known unto us the mystery (or secret) of his will, according to his good pleasure which he hath purposed in himself: that in the dispensation of the fulness of times he might gather together in one all things in Christ, both which are in heaven, and which are on earth . . . "

This gathering together of all things in Christ by God the Father, Paul says, will usher in "the dispensation of the fulness of times"—that is, the period which will mark the culmination and consummation of God's plan that has been gradually maturing throughout all preceding ages.

If we now turn on to Revelation chapter 20, we shall see just how the final resurrection of all the remaining dead will be related to the other parts of God's plan for the consummation of Christ's millennial reign.

In Revelation chapter 20, verses 7 through 10, John portrays the last attempt ever to be made by Satan to oppose the authority of God and of Christ, and to stir up rebellion against it. This occurs at the end of the millennium, and is described by John as follows:

"And when the thousand years are expired, Satan shall be loosed out of his prison,

"And shall go out to deceive the nations which are in the four quarters of the earth, Gog and Magog, to gather them together to battle: the number of whom is as the sand of the sea.

"And they went up on the breadth of the earth, and compassed the camp of the saints about, and the beloved city: and fire came down from God out of heaven, and devoured them.

"And the devil that deceived them was cast into the lake of fire and brimstone, where the beast and the false prophet are, and shall be tormented day and night for ever and ever."

John here uses the phrases "the camp of the saints"

and "the beloved city" to describe the city of Jerusalem and the territory surrounding that. During the period of the millennium Jerusalem will be the earthly centre of Christ's administration and rule over the nations of the earth. During this period Satan will be kept confined as a prisoner in the bottomless pit, but at its close he will be allowed to go free just long enough to stir up this final rebellion amongst the Gentile nations, which will culminate in an attempt to attack Jerusalem. However, God will intervene with fire from heaven; the rebellion will be totally defeated; and Satan himself will be cast into the lake of eternal fire, there to be tormented forever together with the beast (that is, the anti-Christ) and the false prophet, both of whom will already have been cast into the lake of fire at the time of Christ's return to earth and of the commencement of the millennium.

After this, in Revelation chapter 20, verses 11 through 15, John goes on to describe the final resurrection of all the remaining dead:

"And I saw a great white throne, and him that sat on it, from whose face the earth and the heaven fled away; and there was found no place for them.

"And I saw the dead, small and great, stand before God; and the books were opened: and another book was opened, which is the book of life: and the dead were judged out of those things which were written in the books, according to their works.

"And the sea gave up the dead which were in it; and death and hell delivered up the dead which were in them: and they were judged every man according to their works.

"And death and hell were cast into the lake of fire. This is the second death.

"And whosoever was not found written in the book of life was cast into the lake of fire."

In this account we notice that resurrection comes first, then judgment. This same principle is observed at every stage of resurrection. Since it is in their bodies that men have committed acts of good or evil, it is in their bodies also that they must appear before God to hear His judgment upon those acts.

In our previous studies we have already pointed out that all righteous believers who die in the various ages up to the close of the great tribulation will all have been resurrected before the establishment of Christ's millennial kingdom. From this it follows that the great majority of those to be resurrected at the close of the millennium will be the unrighteous dead. In this connection, it is significant that John refers to those resurrected at the close of the millennium as "the dead". He says: "I saw **the dead**, small and great, stand before God." This is different from the language which he uses to describe the resurrection of the righteous dead at the commencement of the millennium. Concerning these he says, in Revelation chapter 20, verse 4, "and they **lived** and reigned with Christ a thousand years." Thus, of the resurrected righteous, John says not merely that they were resurrected, but also that "they **lived**"—they were in the fullest and truest sense "alive". On the other hand, those whom John saw resurrected at the close of the millennium are still "the dead". Although resurrected from the grave in their bodies, they are still spiritually "dead"—"dead in trespasses and sins"—alienated and cut off from the presence and fellowship of God—brought before God for the last time, only to hear His final sentence of condemnation upon them. Thereafter, their destiny is the lake of fire, "the second death", the place of final, eternal banishment from God's presence, the place which offers henceforth no hope either of change or of return.

However, it would appear that amongst those to be resurrected at the close of the millennium there will be a small minority of the righteous. This small minority will be made up of the righteous who died during the period of Christ's millennial reign upon earth.

Concerning this millennial period we find the following prophetic account in Isaiah chapter 65, verse 20: "There shall be no more thence an infant of days, nor an old man that hath not filled his days: for the child shall die an hundred years old; but the sinner being an hundred years old shall be accursed."

The picture here given by Isaiah of life on earth during the millennium indicates that though the span of human life will be greatly extended, nevertheless both the righteous and the sinner will still be subject to death. From this we may conclude that the righteous who die during the millennium will be resurrected at its close, but will not be subject to God's judgment upon the unrighteous who are to be resurrected at this time.

If we now turn again to Revelation chapter 20, we notice the completeness and the finality of the resurrection there recorded by John.

In verse 13 he says: "And the sea gave up the dead which were in it; and death and hell delivered up the dead which were in them: and they were judged every man according to their works."

To this final resurrection of the remaining dead there are no exceptions. It concerns "every man". None is omitted. Every realm of God's created universe is called upon by divine authority to give up the dead which are in it. The three words which John uses in this connection are "the sea", "death", and "hell".

The Greek word here translated "hell" is "hades". This corresponds to the Hebrew word "sheol", used in the Old Testament. "Hades", or "sheol", is a place of temporary confinement for departed spirits, **prior** to their final resurrection and judgment. **After** final reusrrection and judgment, all the unrighteous are consigned to the lake of fire. The usual Hebrew word used in the Old Testament for this lake of fire is not "sheol", but "gehenna".

We see therefore that there is an absolutely clear and complete distinction between "sheol", or "hades", on the one hand, and "gehenna", or "the lake of fire", on the other hand. "Sheol", or "hades", is a place of temporary confinement, to which are consigned the spirits, but not the bodies, of the departed. "Gehenna", or "the lake of fire", is a place of final, unending punishment, to which is consigned, after resurrection, the total personality of every unrighteous person—spirit and soul and body together.

This distinction between "sheol", or "hades", and "the lake of fire," is further brought out by the statement of John in Revelation chapter 20, verse 14: "And death and hell (that is, hades) were cast into the lake of fire." Obviously "hades" cannot be the same as the lake of fire, since "hades", together with "death", is cast into the lake of fire.

Just what is the true nature of "death", and of "hades", as revealed in the New Testament?

Further light upon this question is given in Revelation chapter 6, which contains the famous vision of the four horsemen. Here, concerning the fourth horseman, John says, in Revelation chapter 6, verse 8: "And I looked, and behold a pale horse: and his name that sat on him was Death, and Hell followed with him . . . " Once again, the Greek word here translated "Hell" is "Hades".

It is obvious from this account that both "Death" and "Hades" were here revealed to John as being **persons**. Only a person could sit on a horse; and only another person could follow along with this first one.

This passage therefore greatly increases our understanding of the nature of Death and Hades, as revealed in the scriptures.

In one sense, "death" is a state, or a condition. It is the cessation of life, the experience which results in the separation of the spirit from the body. However, "death" is also a person. "Death" is the dark angel, the minister of Satan, who brings about the condition of physical death, and who separates the spirit from the body.

A similar truth applies also to "hades". In one sense, "hades", is a place of confinement for departed spirits. In another sense, however, "Hades" is a person. "Hades", like "Death", is a dark angel, a minister of Satan, following close upon the heels of "Death", coming to claim the spirits that are separated by Death from the body, and to confine them in the realm of departed spirits from which he receives his name—that is, the realm of "hades".

Thus, "Death" and "Hades" are both alike dark angels, ministers of Satan's infernal kingdom. But the difference between them is this. "Death" has power over men's bodies—power to induce physical death. "Hades" has power over men's spirits—power to confine the spirits of the departed in the realm of hades. For this reason, John saw them moving amongst men in that order—first Death, separating the spirit from the body, and then Hades, taking dominion over the departed spirit.

With this in mind, we are able to understand correctly the statement made by Jesus in John chapter 8, verse 51: "Verily, verily, I say unto you, If a man keep my saying, he shall never **see death**." Jesus does not say here that the believer will not experience physical death. He says that the believer will not "**see death**". He is not referring to the physical condition of death, that results from the separation of the spirit from the body. When He speaks of "seeing death", He is referring to the person of the dark angel, whose name is Death, and to the other dark angel, his companion, whose name is Hades. Jesus means that the spirit of the true believer, on departing from the body, will never come under the dominion of these two dark angels, Death and Hell. Rather, like the poor beggar Lazarus, the departing spirit of the true believer will be met by God's angels—the angels of light—and will by them be escorted into the presence of God.

With this in mind, too, we can properly understand the statement of Paul in First Corinthians chapter 15, verse 26, "The last enemy that shall be destroyed is death;" and also the statement of John in Revelation chapter 20, verse 14, "And death and hell were cast into the lake of fire." In each of these two passages the primary reference is to Death and to Hell as persons, as dark angels, ministers of Satan, and enemies of God and of the human race. The last of all God's enemies to receive the judgment due to him will be Death. Together with Hell, he will be cast into the lake of fire, there to join their master, Satan, and all the rest of Satan's servants and followers, both angelic and human. By this final act of judgment, the last of God's enemies will forever have been banished from His presence.

*　　　*　　　*

In closing this study, let us turn again for a moment to the last sentence with which John concludes his account of the final resurrection. This is found in Revelation chapter 20, verse 15: "And whosoever was not found written in the book of life was cast into the lake of fire."

Side by side with this we may set the familiar words of John chapter 3, verse 16: "For God so loved the world, that he gave his only begotten Son, that whosoever believeth in him should not perish, but have everlasting life."

In these two verses are presented the two great eternal alternatives set before every human soul—either everlasting life, or everlasting fire. In each verse the word "whosoever" is central. Every soul of man must take his place in one or other of these two categories: the "whosoever" of acceptance, or the "whosoever" of rejection.

All those who would escape the lake of everlasting fire have one thing in common: their names are recorded in God's book of life. All those who would enter into everlasting life likewise have one thing in common: a personal faith in Jesus Christ as Saviour and Lord.

Here, then, is the dividing line, the point of decision and separation: a personal faith in Jesus Christ. Only those who have this personal faith in Christ have their names recorded in God's book of life.

This decisive word "whosoever" occurs again, for the last time in the Bible, in Revelation chapter 22, verse 17: "And whosoever will, let him take the water of life freely. Notice those words: "whosoever **will**, let him **take** . . ." These words imply two things: first, a decision; then, an act. First, to "will"; then, to "take".

The acceptance of God's mercy requires positive decision, followed by positive action. To make no decision is, in effect, to make the wrong decision. Not to accept is, in its consequences, the same as to reject.

There is therefore only one way to escape, only one way to everlasting life. That is to make a firm personal decision, and to follow it with positive action: to trust Christ as Saviour, and to serve Him as Lord.

The picture presented in scripture of God's nature and dealings with man is like a coin. It has two opposite sides, which together make up the complete coin. These two sides are clearly presented by Paul in Romans chapter 11, verse 22: "Behold therefore the **goodness** and the **severity** of God." Here are the two sides: "goodness" and "severity": on the one hand, mercy and grace; on the other hand, wrath and judgment.

To efface one side of a coin renders it incomplete and valueless. So it is with the picture of God presented in the Bible. To speak always of "goodness", but never of "severity", to speak always of mercy and grace, but never of wrath and judgment—this is to efface one side of the coin, and to render the Bible's picture of God incomplete and valueless. Those who speak like this are unfaithful to God, and unfair to men. In so doing, they misrepresent God, and mislead men.

To make the coin complete, we must inscribe one "whosoever" upon each side. Upon the side of "goodness" we must inscribe: "Whosoever believeth in him shall not perish, but have everlasting life." Upon the side of "severity", we must inscribe: "Whosoever was not found written in the book of life was cast into the lake of fire."

Then, in presenting the coin to men, we must remind each one that his personal destiny can be settled only by his own personal decision and act. "Whosoever will, let him take . . . "

*   *   *

Our next study will be the last to deal with the theme of the resurrection, and in it we shall consider the nature of the changed and glorified body which each believer will receive at resurrection.

VIII
"With What Body?"

Analogy Of Corn—Fire Distinctive Changes In The Believer's Resurrection Body—The Logical Necessity Of The Doctrine Of The Resurrection

Welcome to the Study Hour.

Our textbook - the Bible.

The study which we shall now bring you is Number 47 in our present series, entitled "Foundations".

We are at present examining that doctrine of the Christian faith which is called, in Hebrews chapter 6, verse 2, "resurrection of the dead".

In our last three studies we have considered in succession the three main phases of the resurrection as stated by the apostle Paul in First Corinthians chapter 15, verses 23 and 24:

First, "Christ the firstfruits"—that is, the resurrection of Christ Himself, together with those of the Old Testament saints who were resurrected with Him.

Second, "they that are Christ's at his coming"—that is, all true Christian believers who have died during the present dispensation, and who will be resurrected at the period of Christ's second coming, prior to the establishment of His millennial kingdom.

Third, "the end"—that is, the final resurrection of all the remaining dead at the close of the millennium.

We shall devote most of our present study to considering what the scripture reveals about the nature of the body with which Christian believers will be resurrected.

In our earlier studies on this subject we have already pointed out that there is direct continuity between the body that dies and is buried, and the body that is later resurrected. The basic material of the body that is to be resurrected is the same as that of the body that is buried. That is to say, resurrection is, in its proper sense, the raising up of **the same body** that was buried, and not the creation of a completely new body.

However, once this fact is established, we must also add that, in the case of the Christian believer, the body that is resurrected undergoes, in this process of resurrection, certain definite and tremendous changes.

This whole question is raised and discussed by Paul in First Corinthians chapter 15, verses 35 through 38, where he says:

"But some man will say, How are the dead raised up? and with what body do they come?

"Thou fool, that which thou sowest is not quickened, except it die:

"And that which thou sowest, thou sowest not that body that shall be, but bare grain, it may chance of wheat, or of some other grain:

"But God giveth it a body as it hath pleased him, and to every seed his own body."

Here Paul uses the analogy of a grain of corn, planted in the ground, to illustrate the relationship between the body that is buried and the body that is raised up in resurrection. Out of this analogy there emerge three facts which may be applied to the resurrection of the body.

First, there is direct continuity between the seed that is planted in the ground and the plant that later grows up out of the ground from that seed. The basic material of the original seed is still contained in the plant that grows up out of that seed.

Second, the plant that grows up out of the original seed undergoes, in that process, certain definite and obvious changes. The outward form and appearance of the new plant is different from that of the original seed.

Third, the nature of the original seed determines the nature of the plant that grows up out of it. Each kind of seed can produce only the kind of plant that is appropriate to it. A seed of wheat can produce only a stalk of wheat; a seed of barley can produce only a stalk of barley.

Let us now apply these three facts, taken from the analogy of a seed, to the nature of the body that is to be resurrected.

First, there is direct continuity of kind between the body that is buried and the body that is resurrected.

Second, the body that is resurrected undergoes, in that process, certain definite and obvious changes. The outward form and appearance of the new, resurrected body is different from that of the original body that was buried.

Third, the nature of the body that is buried determines the nature of the body that is resurrected. There will be a direct logical and causal connection between the condition of the believer in his present earthly existence and the nature of the body with which he will be resurrected.

In First Corinthians chapter 15, verses 39 through 44, Paul goes on to give further details about the nature of the changes that the believer's body will undergo as a result of the resurrection:

"All flesh is not the same flesh: but there is one kind of flesh of men, another flesh of beasts, another of fishes, and another of birds.

"There are also celestial bodies, and bodies terrestrial: but the glory of the celestial is one, and the glory of the terrestrial is another.

"There is one glory of the sun, and another glory of the moon, and another glory of the stars: for one star differeth from another star in glory.

"So also is the resurrection of the dead. It is sown in corruption; it is raised in incorruption:

"It is sown in dishonour; it is raised in glory: it is sown in weakness; it is raised in power:

"It is sown a natural body; it is raised a spiritual body. There is a natural body, and there is a spiritual body."

In order to complete this picture, we should add the statement made by Paul a little further on, in First Corinthians, chapter 15, verse 53:

"For this corruptible must put on incorruption; and this mortal must put on immortality."

This analysis given here by Paul of the nature of the changes that the believer's body will undergo at resurrection may be expressed in the form of a series of statements.

First, Paul points out that, even amongst the bodies of creatures with which we are familiar in the present natural order, there are differences of nature and constitution. He mentions the following main classes: men; animals; fishes;

and birds. This would seem to be in line with the conclusions of modern science that there is no discernible difference in the chemical make-up of the blood of the various different racial groups within the human family; but that there is a difference between the chemical make-up of the blood of human beings and that of other orders of the animal kingdom.

Second, Paul points out that, over and above all bodies of the order with which we are familiar here on earth, there is another different, and higher, order of bodies, which he calls the "celestial", or "heavenly", order. Once again, this is in line with recent scientific discoveries. Science has now succeeded in putting a man into orbit in space; but in order to keep that man alive, science has to confine him in a capsule and to surround him with the atmosphere and conditions of earth. In order to be truly at home any distance from the surface of the earth, man must be equipped with a body of an altogether different order from his present one. But for this he must depend upon God; he cannot do it for himself.

Third, Paul points out that, amongst the various heavenly bodies which we can see—that is, the sun, the moon, and the stars—there are differences of nature and of brightness. The sun produces its own light; the moon merely reflects the light of the sun. Amongst the stars there are many different orders of brightness.

Paul states that the same will be true of the bodies of believers when they are resurrected from the dead. There will be many different orders of glory amongst them.

This is foretold already in the prophecy of the resurrection given in Daniel chapter 12, verses 2 and 3:

"And many of them that sleep in the dust of the earth shall awake, some to everlasting life, and some to shame and everlasting contempt.

"And they that be wise shall shine as the brightness of the firmament; and they that turn many to righteousness as the stars for ever and ever."

Here Daniel foreshows that there will be differences in rewards and in glory amongst the resurrected saints. Those that have been most faithful and most diligent in making known God's truth to others will shine the most brightly.

This picture of the saints resurrected with glorious bodies like those of the stars is also the fulfilment of God's promise to Abraham, recorded in Genesis chapter 15, verse 5, where we read: "And the Lord brought Abraham forth abroad, and said, Look now toward heaven, and tell the stars, if thou be able to number them: and he said unto him, So shall thy seed be."

Included by God amongst Abraham's seed are all those that believe and obey the word of God's promise, just as Abraham himself did—those that accept by faith in their hearts the divine seed of God's Word. In fact, it is this incorruptible seed of God's Word, received by faith in the heart of each believer, that makes possible his resurrection amongst the righteous. In the day of the final fulfilment of God's promise, at the resurrection, all the believers then raised up on the basis of their faith in God's Word will be like the stars that God showed to Abraham—as numerous, as glorious, and as diverse from each other in their glory.

In his analysis of the nature of the believer's resurrection body, Paul closes by listing a series of specific changes that will take place. He actually specifies five such changes.

First, the present body is corruptible—subject to corruption—subject to sickness, decay, and old age. The new body will be incorruptible—free from all these evils.

Second, the present body is mortal—subject to death. The new body will be immortal—incapable of death.

Third, the present body is a body of dishonour. In Philippians chapter 3, verse 21, it is called "our vile body". But a more literal translation of this would be, "the body of our humiliation". Man's present body is the outcome of his sin and disobedience to God. It is a continual source of humiliation—a continual reminder of the fall, and of the physical frailty and insufficiency which result from that. No matter how great may be man's achievements in the realms of art or science, he is continually humbled and brought low by the physical needs and limitations of his body. However, the new resurrection body will be a body of beauty and glory, free from all man's present limitations.

Fourth, the present body is committed to the grave in weakness. The act of burial is the final acknowledgment of man's debt to death; it is the supreme confession of man's weakness. But the new body will be raised up from the grave by the power of almighty God, and the resurrection will thus be a testimony of God's omnipotence, swallowing up the power of death and the grave.

Fifth, the present body is a "natural" body—literally, a "soulish" body. According to the original pattern of God in creation, man was to be a triune being, consisting of spirit, soul and body. Of these three elements, man's spirit was capable of direct communion and fellowship with God, and was intended to control the lower elements of man's nature— that is, the soul and the body. However, as a result of man's yielding to temptation at the fall, these lower elements of his nature—the soul and the body—gained control. This produced far-reaching changes both in man's inner personality and in his physical body. His body became "soulish". Henceforth, its organs and its functions were adapted to the expression and satisfaction of the lower desires of his soul, but were incapable of fully expressing the higher aspirations of his spirit. In some sense, this "soulish" body is a prison— a place of confinement and restriction—for man's spirit. However, the new resurrection body will be "spiritual". It will be perfectly adapted to express and fulfil the highest aspirations of man's spirit. Clothed in this new body, the spirit will once again be the controlling element, and the whole personality of the resurrected believer will function in harmony and perfection under the spirit's control.

Finally, in First Corinthians chapter 15, verses 47 through 49, Paul sums up the differences between the old and the new body by contrasting the body of Adam with that of Christ, and by saying that the resurrected body of the believer will be similar to that of the Lord Himself.

"The first man is of the earth, earthy: the second man is the Lord from heaven.

"As is the earthy, such are they also that are earthy: and as is the heavenly, such are they also that are heavenly.

"And as we have borne the image of the earthy, we shall also bear the image of the heavenly."

That is to say, man's present body is similar, in its earthly nature, to the body of the first created man, Adam, from whom all other men are descended. But the resurrection body of the believer will be similar to that of Christ, who, through the new creation, has become the head of a new race, in which are included all those redeemed through faith in Him from sin and its consequences.

This truth concerning the body of the resurrected believer is stated again by Paul in Philippians chapter 3, verses 20 and 21, where he says:

"For our conversation is in heaven; from whence also we look for the Saviour, the Lord Jesus Christ:

"Who shall change our vile body, that it may be fashioned like unto his glorious body, according to the working whereby he is able even to subdue all things unto himself."

Translated more literally, this last verse states that Christ is able to transform "the body of our humiliation so that it becomes similar in form to the body of his glory."

The apostle John also states the same truth concerning the transformation of the believer at the return of Christ in his First Epistle, chapter 3, verse 2, where he says: "Beloved, now are we the sons of God, and it doth not yet appear what we shall be: but we know that, when he shall appear, we shall be like him; for we shall see him as he is."

In First Corinthians chapter 15, verses 51 through 53, Paul indicates that even those Christians who are alive at Christ's return, and who therefore will not need to be resurrected, will at that time undergo a similar instantaneous and miraculous change in their bodies. He says:

"Behold, I show you a mystery; we shall not all sleep, but we shall all be changed,

"In a moment, in the twinkling of an eye, at the last trump: for the trumpet shall sound, and the dead shall be raised incorruptible, and we shall be changed.

"For this corruptible must put on incorruption, and this mortal must put on immortality."

Here, where Paul says, "We shall not all sleep," he means, "We shall not all die." Then he goes on to say: "but we shall all be changed." In other words, all true believers, whether resurrected, or raptured alive, will undergo the same instantaneous and miraculous change in their bodies.

Concerning the nature of Christ's own body after His resurrection, the record of the Gospels gives us certain interesting indications. It would appear that He was no longer subject to those limitations of time and space with which we are familiar in our present earthly body. He could appear, or disappear, at will; He could be in one place at one moment, and in another place some distance away at the next moment. He could also pass from earth to heaven and back again at will. In these, and in other respects which are perhaps not yet revealed, the body of the redeemed believer, after resurrection or rapture, will be like that of his Lord.

So far we have spoken only about the resurrection body of the redeemed believer. What about the unrighteous? those who are not redeemed? those that die in their sins?

The scripture reveals clearly that these too, in their own order, will be resurrected for judgment and for punishment. With what kind of bodies will they be clothed at their resurrection?

To this question it would appear that no clear answer, or even indication, is found in the Bible. We must therefore be content to leave it unanswered.

*   *   *

In concluding this final study on the resurrection of the dead, we should do well to consider briefly why this doctrine is important. There are three main reasons why the doctrine of the resurrection occupies a special, central place in the Christian faith.

The first reason is that the resurrection is God's own vindication of Jesus Christ Himself. This is stated by Paul in Romans chapter 1, verse 4, where he says that Christ was "declared to be the Son of God with power, according to the spirit of holiness, by the resurrection from the dead . . . "

Previously, Christ had been brought before two human courts—first, the religious court of the Jewish Council, and then the secular court of the Roman Governor, Pontius Pilate. Both these courts had rejected the claim of Jesus to be the Son of God, and had condemned Him to death. Furthermore, both these courts had united in seeking to prevent any breaking open of the grave of Jesus. To this end, the Jewish Council had provided their special seal, and the Roman Governor had provided an armed guard of soldiers. However, on the third day God Himself intervened. The seal was broken; the armed guard was paralysed; and Jesus Christ came forth from the tomb. By this act, God reversed the decisions of the Jewish Council and the Roman Governor, and He publicly vindicated the claim of Christ to be the sinless Son of God.

The second main reason for the importance of the resurrection is that it is the sure seal upon God's offer of forgiveness and salvation to every repentant sinner who will put his faith in Christ. In Romans chapter 4, verse 25, Paul says that Christ was "delivered for our offences, and was **raised again for our justification.**" This shows that the sinner's justification is dependent upon Christ being raised again from the dead. Had Christ remained upon the cross, or in the tomb, God's promise to the sinner of salvation and eternal life could never have been fulfilled. It is only the risen Christ, received and confessed by faith, who brings to the sinner pardon, peace, eternal life, and victory over sin.

Paul states the same truth again in Romans chapter 10, verse 9, where he says: "If thou shalt confess with thy mouth the Lord Jesus,—or Jesus as Lord,—and shalt believe in thine heart that God hath raised him from the dead, thou shalt be saved." Here salvation is stated to be dependent upon two things: first, openly confessing Jesus as Lord; second, believing in the heart that God raised Jesus from the dead. Thus, saving faith includes faith in the resurrection. There can be no salvation for those who do not believe in the resurrection of Christ.

Logic and intellectual honesty permit no other conclusion. If Christ is not risen from the dead, then He has no power to pardon or to save the sinner. But if He is risen, as the scripture states, then this is logical proof of His power to pardon and to save. This consequence of Christ's resurrection is clearly set forth in Hebrews chapter 7, verse 25: "Wherefore **he is able to save** them to the uttermost that come unto God by him, **seeing he ever liveth** to make intercession for them."

The absolute, logical necessity of Christ's resurrection as a basis of God's offer of salvation is stated again by Paul in First Corinthains chapter 15. In verse 14 he says: "If Christ be not risen, then is our preaching vain, and your faith is also vain." Again, in verse 17: "If Christ be not raised, your faith is vain: ye are yet in your sins."

The condition of contemporary Christendom abundantly confirms these plain statements of scripture. Those theologians who reject the personal, physical resurrection of Christ may moralise and theorise as much as they please, but one thing they never come to know in personal experience: the peace and the joy of sins forgiven.

Finally, the third reason for the importance of the resurrection is that it constitutes the culmination of all our hopes, as Christians, and the supreme goal of our life of faith here on earth. In Philippians chapter 3, verses 10 through 12, Paul declares his own personal attitude towards the resurrection as the supreme purpose and consummation of all his earthly endeavours. Speaking of the motivating purpose of his life as a Christian, he says:

"That I may know him (Christ), and **the power of his resurrection**, and the fellowship of his sufferings, being made conformable unto his death;

"If by any means I might attain unto the resurrection of the dead.

"Not as though I had already attained, either were already perfect: but I follow after, if that I may apprehend that for which also I am apprehended of Christ Jesus."

Notice particularly those two phrases: "that I may know the power of his resurrection"; and again, "if **by any means** I might attain unto the resurrection of the dead." Paul did not intend to let anything in this world prevent him from attaining to the consummation of all his beliefs and labours— the resurrection of the dead. In this respect, the attitude of every Christian believer should be the same as that of Paul.

If there is no resurrection, then the Christian faith and the Christian life are a pathetic deception. Paul sums this up in First Corinthians chapter 15, verse 19: "If in this life only we have hope in Christ, we are of all men most miserable." But if we believe in the resurrection, then to attain personally to it must be the supreme aim and endeavour of every sincere Christian.

*   *   *

In our next studies in this series we shall go on to consider the last of the six great foundation doctrines of the Christian faith—that is, "eternal judgment".*

**These studies are published separately as Book VII of the "Foundations" series, under the title: "ETERNAL JUDGMENT". See back cover of this book.*